SOLITARY ACTION

SOLITARY ACTION

Acting on Our Own in Everyday Life

Ira J. Cohen

OXFORD
UNIVERSITY PRESS

Oxford University Press is a department of the University of Oxford. It furthers
the University's objective of excellence in research, scholarship, and education
by publishing worldwide. Oxford is a registered trade mark of Oxford University
Press in the UK and in certain other countries

Published in the United States of America by Oxford University Press
198 Madison Avenue, New York, NY 10016, United States of America

© Oxford University Press 2016

Library of Congress Cataloging-in-Publication Data

Cohen, Ira J.
Solitary action : acting on our own in everyday life / Ira J. Cohen.
p.   cm.
Includes bibliographical references and index.
ISBN 978-0-19-025857-3 (hardcover : alk. paper) 1. Social distance.
2. Social interaction. 3. Solitude. 4. Social psychology. I. Title.
HM1131.C64 2016
302—dc23
2015007684

1 3 5 7 9 8 6 4 2

Printed in the United States of America on acid-free paper

To Elizabeth, For Reggie

CONTENTS

ACKNOWLEDGMENTS

The theme of this book originated with my sense of a significant blind spot in theories of social interaction. It has always seemed to me that George Herbert Mead, Harold Garfinkel, and Erving Goffman not only founded the study of social interaction, but established the parameters for the field that have continued to shape how we think about interaction right up to our most recent work. However, despite their deep insights into what Goffman (1983) aptly termed "the interaction order," it struck me that they grasped only one segment of what people do in everyday life. To read their works, one might come away with the notion that people continuously engage in conversation, games, and other forms of interpersonal behavior. But, without gainsaying the prevalence or significance of interpersonal behavior in everyday life, the founders of the sociology of interaction and the generations of scholars whom they influenced overlooked or set aside the numerous activities people perform each day on their own. We may be a social species, but we can and do work and play by ourselves. A complete sociology of everyday life needed conceptual means to take activity beyond the boundaries of the interaction order into account. In this book I develop the concept of solitary action to fill this need. Even in the initial stage of writing this book the idea of solitary action proved sociologically fruitful in that once I adopted it I began to see more going on in everyday life than I had noticed in the past. It was like changing focus on a camera so that all sorts of behavior that previously appeared in the blur of the background suddenly appeared vivid and well defined. Ultimately, this vision enabled me to classify and identify four different forms of solitary action that I now refer to as: peripatetics, regimens, engrossments and reflexives. But no matter how original these concepts may be, I could not have conceived the nature and elements of solitary action without the lessons I have learned from Goffman, Garfinkel, and Mead.

During the course of writing this book it has been my good fortune to have two of the greatest friends I can imagine within or beyond intellectual life, namely Eviatar Zerubavel and John Levi Martin. It may seem inconsistent for the author of a book on solitary action to describe the social support he received from colleagues. But of course all authors write mainly by themselves. Support from others arrives when their attention is not fixed on the page.

I owe an unusual debt to Eviatar Zerubavel, my friend and colleague at Rutgers. I might never have completed this project were it not for Eviatar's unflagging support, generous encouragement, and astute readings of numerous drafts. But there is more. In the acknowledgments to his book *Social Structures* (2009, p. vii), John Levi Martin thanked Eviatar, inter alia, for counseling John to follow his instincts in his choice of themes. Eviatar gave me similar advice. It was the example Eviatar set that brought the words home. Eviatar is that rare breed of scholar who merges an endlessly original sociological imagination with the discipline that is the mark of a true intellectual. Though we write on very different themes, he has been an abiding influence on how I wrote this book.

John Levi Martin is a second member of that rare species of social theorist who merge imagination and vision with the highest standards of intellectual discipline and integrity. Like many, I have always been impressed by his sociological range and originality. Though I solicited John's reactions when I sent him a preliminary draft of a key chapter in this book, I had no expectation for the deep and detailed comments he sent. More importantly, John seemed intuitively to understand where I was trying to go with my ideas. His understanding of my project was a gift of enormous significance to me then and now. I continued to send chapters to John as the work moved ahead and he came back each time with detailed critical comments of the highest order. John has been a dedicated supporter of this book in many other ways. It is my great fortune to count John not only as a colleague but also as a friend.

I have a number of other friends to thank for their encouragement and support. Mary Rogers was my co-author on another project, my good friend and much more: a scholar, an activist, and a person deeply sensitive to other's needs. She died way too young but will never be forgotten by all who knew her. I must also thank Rob Stones, who has been my friend for many years. Rob's generosity at a critical point late in the production of this book means a great deal to me.

I have given papers based upon various iterations of this book at too many professional meetings to mention each one individually. However, I must make three special acknowledgments and thanks here for the opportunity and funding to present my work in distant settings. First, to Iago Kachkachishvili for inviting me to spend a week, along with several Rutgers faculty, lecturing at the Department of Sociology, Tblisi State University in the

Republic of Georgia. My thanks to the Open Society Foundation for funding this trip. Second, to Emiliano Grimaldi and Roberto Serpieri for the invitation and funding for a week spent lecturing and teaching at the Department of Sociology, University of Naples Federico II in 2008. Finally, to Sandro Segre of the Department of Sociology, University of Genoa, for organizing and funding a series of presentations of my work on solitary action in 2009 at the Department of Sociology at the Catholic University of the Sacred Heart of Milan, the Department of Sociology at the University of Genoa, the Department of Sociology at the University of Milan Boccoca, and the Department of Sociology at the University of Pisa. The comments and reactions I received on these trips contributed in many ways to the development of this book.

I also offer great thanks to colleagues and friends who read and commented on earlier drafts of various chapters in this book. They include: Deborah Carr, Karen Cerulo, David Gibson, E. Doyle McCarthy, Michal Pagis, Bryan Turner, Norbert Wiley, John Urry, Richard Williams, and Yael Zerubavel. I want to thank the many cohorts of graduate students in the Graduate Program in Sociology at Rutgers University, those who offered comments on this project as well as those who took my classes in Contemporary Social Theory. Students seldom realize how much their teachers learn from them. That certainly has been true for me.

It is my great pleasure to acknowledge Clay Hartjen, my friend, and Chair of the Department of Sociology and Anthropology at Rutgers Newark. Over the course of many years Clay built a department based on goodwill and mutual respect. Clay has been both supportive and patient as I completed this work. My thanks also to Sherri-Ann Butterfield who followed Clay Hartjen as department chair, sustaining and improving upon his legacy.

I want especially to thank James Cook, my editor at Oxford University Press. His astute counsel proved crucial in seeing this book to print. I could not have asked for, or expected, better support of an editor. I am also grateful to the Oxford production team lead by the very able senior project manager, B. Gogulanathan, the copy editor, Susie Hara, who devoted such meticulous attention to my manuscript, and to Amy Klopfenstein, sociology and criminology editorial assistant, who handled all of my queries with such professional aplomb. Cyril A. Ghosh carved out time from his own academic writing to expertly create the index for this book. In the 10 years that I have known Cyril he has worked on academic publications with all three members of my family and in the process has become like family to us.

A special thanks to Mobus Operandi and all the gang at Moby B's. There is really no greater friend in the world and no place as welcoming with warmth, wit, and imagination.

It is not every father who has the opportunity to thank his daughter for her professional support. However, it is with pride that I thank Professor Elizabeth Feiner Cohen for her encouragement and her reading and astute comments on several drafts of this book. In an ideal world our desks would sit side by side.

Finally, my love and gratitude to my wife, Reggie Feiner Cohen. She has contributed to this book in more ways than I can recount and has made all the difference in my life. W. H. Auden once said that a lifelong happy marriage is one of the greatest gifts life has to offer. Auden was right.

SOLITARY ACTION

Chapter 1

Introduction

INTRODUCING SOLITARY ACTION

For four hundred years readers have been drawn to Daniel Defoe's tales of Robinson Crusoe, an unexceptional English man marooned in solitary isolation on a tropical desert island. Finding himself alone until the latter years of his stay when he meets an island native he calls Friday, Crusoe proceeds to build a full way of life for himself complete with fixed routines, practical improvisations, and occasional crises that he surmounts with extraordinary feats of ingenuity and self-reliance. *Robinson Crusoe* is a fantasy of course. To enjoy his story, readers must suspend their disbelief. Yet, like many other fantasies, Defoe's novel expands upon a phenomenon that is a commonplace feature of our everyday lives. That feature is what I term *solitary action*, which may be understood in brief as any kind of activity or behavior individuals undertake without intervention by anyone else during the course of the activity. We may not believe that Defoe's protagonist flourished for such a prolonged period of time by means of solitary action alone. But we are quite familiar with things we, and those around us, do by ourselves. Indeed, it is because of our familiarity with doing things on our own that we are willing to suspend our disbelief in Defoe's imaginary tale and it is this familiarity as well that leads us to admire his protagonist's solitary virtuosity.

But in saying that we are familiar with solitary action I do not mean to say that we are fully aware of what we do by ourselves. This is so in two different respects. First, while my fellow sociologists have made extraordinary progress in the study of how individuals engage in social interaction, they have seldom acknowledged that there is an entire realm of behaviors in which people engage when they are not involved in interpersonal encounters. There are several reasons for this sociological neglect about which I will have more to say in chapter 2. But second, there is a widespread tendency in our culture at large to overlook the fact that solitary activity can be as absorbing in its own ways as socializing with others. Indeed, as Henry David Thoreau notes in his journals composed at Walden Pond ([1854] 1992, pp. 91–92), the same people who do a great deal by themselves may fail to make sense of the solitary activity performed by others.

> The farmer can work alone in the field or the woods all day, hoeing or chopping, and not feel lonesome, because he is employed; but when he comes home at night he cannot sit down in a room alone, at the mercy of his thoughts, but must be where he can "see the folks" and recreate . . . and hence he wonders how the student can sit alone in the house all night and most of the day without ennui and "the blues;" but he does not realize that the student, though in his house, is still at work in his field and chopping in his woods, as the farmer in his. . . .

Notice that Thoreau observes not only that his farmer cannot understand how the student can work on his own for long periods of time, but also the reason for the farmer's surprise. The farmer fails to recognize that the student is not simply alone with his thoughts but is engaged and absorbed by his studies.

This sense of behavioral engagement in solitary activity will play an integral role in the concept of solitary action that I develop in this book. But by way of introduction, it is enough to simply look around and take note of the kinds of things people do by themselves, which as Thoreau suggests we may be prone to overlook or disregard.

Consider familiar scenes of passengers in waiting areas at airports or railway terminals. Some may chat with others either in person or by phone. But once they are seated, many passengers, as if on cue, immediately retrieve reading materials, music players, knitting projects, office documents, school assignments, or electronic devices on which they may play games, watch movies, or surf the web. Indeed, even in this electronic age is there a busy transportation terminal anywhere in the world that lacks a shop well stocked with materials people can use to do things by themselves? Now move to a very different setting, the modern office suite wherein today we find offices or (regrettably, but quite often) office cubicles populated by employees doing various work assignments on their own. A person performing spreadsheet calculations may be unaware of a person nearby drafting a proposal or someone else entering data on electronic forms. Libraries, of course, are well known as venues for solitary activity. At the same time that one person in a reading room may be studying for an exam, another may be studying documents from the archives that may change how we interpret historically important individuals or events. There are numerous other public sites where we find people engaged in solitary activities, from exercise gyms and jogging trails to secluded park benches and crowded urban streets. We also should not ignore our homes, where at various times of the day individuals find themselves alone or claim zones of solitude in order to do some housework or homework or recreate by themselves. Even a kitchen table in a crowded apartment can be a venue for solitary activity, provided that while one individual acts, no one else intervenes.

Solitary action possesses traits that quicken the sociological imagination. We find here an extensive range of behaviors we ordinarily disattend that upon reflection appear interwoven into the basic fabric of everyday life. My purpose in this book is to introduce and explore this hitherto half-hidden realm of human behavior as a suitable subject for sociological enquiry. In this sense, I embark here on a voyage of sociological discovery. Though I write with a social theorist's concern for conceptual definitions, classifications, and the like, I do not want to weigh down discussion with unnecessary theoretical baggage. For example, as I construct my framework for the analysis of solitary action in chapters 3–5, I have relied on substantive illustrations to bring conceptual points to life while refraining from the kinds of Talmudic exegeses and parochial debates that sometimes make audiences with a more general interest in the subject at hand feel disoriented and unwelcome. Chapter 2, which poses the question of why social thinkers have ignored or dismissed solitary action, is a notable exception here. However, readers will still find substantive examples along the way and if the chapter clears some theoretical ground for solitary action it will have done its job.

SOLITARY ACTION: A CATEGORICAL DEFINITION

It is one thing to simply define solitary action as things we do by ourselves and another to give this broad category of behavior the serious sociological attention it has previously lacked. Some questions need to be addressed from the start in order to erect a viable framework that zeroes in on a subject matter that can be difficult to specify. Consider a more specific definition of solitary action than the brief definition introduced above. Let me add that like all opening definitions, this one implies an entire agenda of issues that remain to be addressed, some in this chapter and others in chapters yet to come. Here is the definition: *Solitary actions are sequences of behavior enacted by individuals with no input or interference by anyone else from one move in the sequence to the next.* Here are a few more examples of solitary action to bring this definition to life and to indicate the extraordinary diversity of activities that this definition subsumes. Thus, to anticipate a detailed pair of examples at the beginning of chapter 3, playing solitaire proceeds via a highly structured sequence of moves, while solo jazz improvisation proceeds via a sequence with a much looser structure that leaves numerous alternative pathways to develop and explore. Likewise, a jigsaw puzzle requires an exact number of successful moves in order to complete a predetermined image, while a painting may take an indefinite number of moves to develop an image that no one, including the painter herself, clearly had in mind from the start. Some solitary actions such as writing a sonnet require intellectual discipline and linguistic skill. Others, like driving a bus, require eye–hand coordination and practical knowledge learned on the job.

The diversity of solitary activities made manifest here can be multiplied at great length. But the foregoing examples suffice to suggest that a modicum of elasticity be introduced to the definition above. First, any specified form of solitary action may take a smaller or larger number of moves to complete, or in some cases a given form of solitary action may go on indefinitely. Thus, making an entry on one's electronic calendar may take only two or three moves, or a dozen if you prefer to count each keystroke in the entry as a separate step. Conversely, some projects such as building a software program or writing a novel may require more moves than it can be reasonably expected for anyone to observe and record. As for solitary activities that can go on indefinitely, one need only think of Leonardo da Vinci's adage (also widely attributed to others) that: "Art is never finished, only abandoned." But the same can be said of many activities that lack the prestige of fine art, for example, playing slot machines, surfing the web, searching for something one has lost. The second bit of elasticity suggested here refers to the fact that some solitary activities take much longer than others to complete. Filling the blanks in a short bureaucratic form may take only a few minutes, while writing a novel or preparing a graduate dissertation may take many years. Obviously, longer solitary projects will be broken up into intervals and routines during which individuals alternatively pursue developments in the solitary project at hand and then disengage to do other things, whether alone or in the company of others.

Finally, we should allow for activities that hold our attention episodically, that is, intermittently holding our interest and then letting it go. This possibility will expand into a discussion of a form of solitary action I term peripatetics in chapter 4. But consider by way of example various forms of browsing activity, for example, reading a magazine or a news website, searching for items of interest on a solo safari to a shopping mall, or rummaging through old items in one's attic or storage space. During some intervals one comes up empty. But there are more or less frequent times when an item attracts our interest and holds our attention for a while.

One of the most significant implications of the definition of solitary action at hand is that we are not necessarily engaged in solitary activity simply because we happen to be uninvolved in interpersonal conduct. It is what we do by ourselves, and not the simple fact of being alone that determines if we are engaged in solitary action. There are, in fact, various ways in which we may be alone yet not engaged in solitary action as I define the term here. To take the most obvious example, it seems nonsensical to propose that we engage in solitary action in our sleep. Why? Because with the possible exception of those who report they can intervene and alter their own dreams, we lack any control of ourselves during this solitary period in our daily lives. Simply put: we lack any agency when we sleep. But sleep is not alone in this regard. Consider the category of reactions to bodily distress. Are these examples of solitary action? Migraine sufferers may retreat to dark, silent spots where they remain alone and very still in order to limit the extent of their pain, but they are so driven by their distress that they would seem to lack any agency in the exercise of their own behavior. Likewise, a person who stubs one's toe alone in a room and then curses out loud at the fast and sharp pain can only be said to engage in an action under an excessively broad definition of the term. Thus, physically compelled behavior lacks the agency to qualify as action in that the individual has little control over what he or she does. We should also be quite cautious of the kinds of images, intuitions, and memories that float or flash into our minds in an uncontrollable way. Spontaneous daydreams, reminiscences, and flashes of unexpected insight and imagination all may be invaluable as grounds for creative projects or other things we do by ourselves or with others. But they are not solitary actions because we can neither start nor develop them as we like. I shall have more to say on spontaneous states of mind in a discussion of what I term mental peripatetics in chapter 4 and a discussion of epiphanies in chapter 5. For now it suffices to note that there are both physical and mental forms of behavior over which we have little control that fall beyond the ambit of solitary action as I define the phenomenon here.

SOLITARY ACTIVITIES AS UNITS OF ANALYSIS

Whatever unit of analysis is chosen at the head of a study inevitably shapes all that follows. Yet, while well-crafted treatises have been written to justify or legitimate the choice of one unit of analysis rather than another, in the end there are no unassailable grounds on which the choice can be made. Within realistic and reasonable limits, units of analysis are a matter of theoretical preference. In this book I choose to conceive solitary action as forms of activity, that is, an intrinsically related series of moves enacted through the exercise of human agency. To focus on forms of activity as units of analysis implies nothing about how often such forms occur. The process of producing an invention may happen only once and never again. Conversely, an untold number of elementary school children—past, present, and future—study by themselves in broadly similar ways for standardized arithmetic tests during the course of any given academic year. The fact that one activity is unique and the other is ubiquitous does not affect their common status as forms of solitary action. Forms of solitary behavior conceived as units of analysis may vary along other dimensions as well. Indeed, as readers will see in chapters 4 and 5, two variables in particular, the degree of structuration and the degree to which a given form of activity holds the actor's attention, are pivotal criteria I use to classify four common forms of solitary action.

The idea of adopting forms of activity as units of analysis in the study of solitary action may strike some readers as an unusual move. Under some definitions the term solitary may refer to an individual who is separate from others. This definition differs from the sense of solitary as a condition in which an individual does something on his or her own, which is how I mean to use the term here. To define solitary with reference to the individual suggests a theoretical focus on the actor, a self-conscious person who is subjectively aware of what he or she is doing now, has done in the past, or intends to do in future. Individualist orientations can be hard to resist. They can easily create a kind of intellectual centripetal force that makes the study of solitary action from the standpoint of the individual seem like an inevitable choice. This is surely the case in psychology and neurobiology, as well as in many philosophical traditions, ancient and modern alike. Closer to home, the sociology of action may well have begun with Max Weber's famous definition of action as the subjective meaning an individual ascribes to her or his behavior. Then too, rational choice theorists inject utilitarian individualism into their sociological inquiries. And new ways of conceiving individuals as actors in social circumstances continue to arise. The latest of these theories focuses on the dialogical relations between self and society as well as the internal reflections of the self upon its social circumstances and activities.[1] In recent years Margaret Archer and Norbert Wiley have broken new ground in this domain, with Archer (2003) focusing on internal conversation and Wiley (2006) on inner speech.

Yet, without gainsaying the study of individuals as actors, the process of acting can get lost along the way. It is one thing, after all, to say that an author is writing a novel and another to say how our author works at the novel day by day. In the first case we learn about the author's thoughts, feelings, and intentions

---

1. It may forestall some conceptual confusion later on to note that when I speak of "contextual reflexivity" in chapters 4 and 5. I refer to the ways in which any move in a line of solitary activity relies on the context previously established in that line and the possibilities that move creates for moves yet to come. Thus, "contextual reflexivity" does not refer to either internal or external relations between self and society, though, by the same token, the salience of questions regarding self–society relations is in no sense denied.

with reference to her or his writing, whereas in the second case we learn how an author moves from one paragraph to the next, the problems that arise and how they are resolved, the way the narrative is organized, and how the novel is revised. Recall here Defoe's accounts of Robinson Crusoe's fantastic improvisations. The fact that Crusoe as an individual was desperate to survive in an inhospitable environment is a crucial element of the story, of course. But we keep reading to see what he does and how he does it. To say that a shipwrecked individual will do whatever he can to stay alive hardly begins to tell the tale. So it is what people do, not what they mean or intend that matters here, an idea Erving Goffman (1967, p. 3) once condensed in a lapidary phrase: "Not, then, men and their moments. Rather moments and their men."

SOLITARY ACTION AND THE INTERACTION ORDER

To draw Goffman into the discussion here is in no way coincidental. Indeed, Goffman, his contemporary Harold Garfinkel, and their predecessor George Herbert Mead are largely responsible for introducing forms of behavior as units of analysis in the sociology of action, a domain of inquiry Goffman (1983) dubbed the "interaction order." I am deeply indebted to the visionary insights of these three pioneers for inspiration and conceptual tools, without which I would have been unable to envision this study. I do not believe I am alone in these debts. It has been many decades since the most provocative and groundbreaking of their works first appeared, yet their sense of activities as units of analysis and their respective models for how forms of behavior should be studied continue to shape the ways in which we think about action today. But my debts to those who took it upon themselves to make the interaction order a suitable field for sociological inquiry come with a very obvious asterisk, of course. Solitary action and social interaction are, by definition, mutually exclusive phenomena. One cannot simultaneously participate in a sustained conversation and carry out a sustained series of moves by oneself. Moreover, as I will discuss further in chapter 2, Goffman, Garfinkel, and Mead, each in a distinctive way, relegated solitary behavior to the status of a trivial concern and for the most part left things people do by themselves out of their accounts. So, if the progenitors of modern studies of interaction have little to say about solitary action, and if the two forms of action are incommensurable in any event, we are left to ask: how do these two forms of behavior relate to one another? How do they differ; what do they share in common?

Answers to these questions require an initial acknowledgment that we are dealing with two forms of human behavior. A taxonomic metaphor seems almost inevitable here: that is, solitary action and social interaction are two species of a single genus. But it is simplistic, not to say reductionist, to differentiate the two solely in terms of the number of people involved. When people interact, they create conditions that are impossible for people to generate when they do things on their own. Three overlapping differences stand out. First, as Harold Garfinkel was the first to observe, social interaction continuously creates a context that no single participant can direct or control. Even within a two-party chat, the subject matter and tone of the exchange may shift dramatically from one turn of talk to the next. Staying abreast of the topic at hand and finding ways to steer the course of discussion in one direction rather than another are essential skills here. A pivotal insight in analysis of solitary action I shall develop in chapter 3 is that solitary action involves context creation to the same extent as social interaction. The difference is that the entire sequence of behavior is carried out by a single agent. The constraints or requirements for improvisation in context formation will vary a great deal between different forms of solitary behavior. But no other person on the scene will alter the context from one move to the next.

The second and third differences between solitary action and social interaction are so closely interrelated that they must be paired together. As Erving Goffman demonstrated on numerous occasions, social interaction is structured in part by implicit norms of etiquette that require all participants to respect one another's dignity and rights during the course of the exchange. Whatever the meaning or purpose of the exchange, the encounter itself has a moral order of its own. This implicit moral etiquette is lacking in solitary action. So too is a third difference. The implicit moral rules of interaction license participants to monitor one another's behavior and impose appropriate sanctions when infractions are observed. No analogies for social etiquette and interpersonal surveillance exist with regard to solitary action. Solitary actors may be tightly constrained by the demands of the activity at hand, for example by the program of a video game or the challenge of a mathematical problem. But the solitary actor has no need to attend to the dignity or rights of others on the scene. Of course, just because activity is enacted apart from others does not necessarily indicate the absence of more distant obligations and delayed sanctions beyond the local setting. Many different occupations require solitary kinds of work, including everything from truck driving to artwork. Similarly, in any long-standing couple or family, many things are done by one party in the absence of others. But at work or at home, there will be others who have certain expectations that an activity will be properly performed. This is not always the case. Some forms of solitary activity afford the individual opportunities for autonomous initiatives and personal indulgence. But the point here is that solitary action may be subject to delayed surveillance and sanction even though no social obligations must be met while the activity is underway.

Finally, on a more methodological note I should indicate one way in which I have followed Garfinkel and Goffman's lead. As Goffman (1967, pp. 1–3) indicates in the passage that closes with his preference to study "moments and their men," inquiries into forms of human behavior are best carried out with as little psychological baggage as possible. Garfinkel (and Harvey Sacks, 1970, p. 345) invoked similar brackets around states of mind among other items they include under the heading of "ethnomethodological indifference." Of course, as Goffman was wise to observe, one cannot completely exclude states of mind from any study of human behavior. But in this study I have bracketed off one sphere of mental life, namely subjective motivation. These brackets on motivation follow logically in the shift from the analysis of individuals to the analysis of action mentioned above. However, there is a certain advantage to these brackets that I spell out in later chapters that merits at least an anticipatory note here. Simply put, one of the insights I found most intriguing in thinking about solitary action is that to a varying extent certain forms of solitary action have the capacity, as they are being performed, to involve and hold the attention of the actor. One of my reasons for analyzing context formation in the game of solitaire is that it illustrates this holding power to good effect. However, as will become quite evident in forms of solitary action I analyze under the heading of regimens in chapter 4, some forms of solitary action are poorly suited to involve the individual's attention at all. It may seem counterintuitive to speak of the action involving the individual rather than the individual investing herself in behavior. Bracketing questions of motivation, interest, and will provides the analytic freedom to entertain this less obvious point.

SOLITARY ACTION AND SOCIETY AT LARGE

Experienced readers in the sociology of action generally understand from the start that the subject matter at hand will focus on moves, sequences, practices, and projects on a level of inquiry that brackets the questions about society at large that so-called grand theory prefers to address. Nevertheless, certain questions uniquely arise because individuals engaged in solitary action do so by themselves, unaccompanied by others. Let me briefly indicate where I stand on two of these issues here.

The first may be framed in normative terms or as a question about human nature, depending on your point of view. The question is: Does a study of solitary action necessarily imply a concept of human nature in which individuals naturally gravitate toward acting by themselves or does it imply a normative preference for solitary behavior? The question is not entirely hypothetical. There is a well-known, broadly influential tradition within utilitarian philosophy from which positive inferences about solitary action might be drawn. Of course, as I shall indicate in chapter 2, there are also numerous philosophers and social theorists who subscribe to the notion that human beings are inherently social creatures or that somehow we should prefer to be with others rather than being alone. I see no reason to accept either of these positions, nor do I write about solitary action with a normative preference for behavior of this kind. I believe that as a species we do not necessarily prefer or gravitate to solitude or sociability. We are no more stray cats or lone wolves who have no use for living in a group than we are schools of fish or colonies of ants that must continuously comingle or die. Thus, to study solitary action is not to make a claim about human nature, nor to make a normative case for the merits of doing things by oneself. We study it because we know much less about it than other forms of human behavior and everyday life.

The second question arises because a concern with solitary action may seem to suggest an interest in the culture of modernity. It is well known, after all, that modern culture encourages self-sufficiency, self-expression, and individual achievement, all of which may involve solitary activities of many and varied kinds. Moreover, as Eric Klinenberg amply demonstrates in *Going Solo* (2012), there is a quite noticeable trend among various classes in modern cultures over the last few decades to dwell apart from others. Though few of Klinenberg's subjects are latter-day hermits, they do appear to do more things by themselves than their counterparts who live with others at home. The trend toward people doing more things by themselves may make a study of solitary action more relevant today than it might have been during the 1950s and 60s, when cultural norms and conventional relationships left less time to do things by oneself than would appear to be the case today. But the twenty-first century is hardly unique in terms of solitary pursuits. During the 1980s five massive volumes of essays were published in France, each edited by eminent historians, and each devoted to the history of private life in a specific era from antiquity to modern times. Though not exclusively dedicated to the study of solitary practices per se, examples of things pre-modern people did by themselves are easy to find (see Aires and Duby, 1987–1991). I have no doubt that many culturally specific varieties of solitary action may be found in any civilization, culture, or historical era one cares to name. Nonetheless, the enactment of solitary actions and not their cultural prevalence or their historical significance is my main concern. Indeed, if the concepts I develop in chapters 3–5 prove useful, they should apply just as well to the analysis of solitary actions wherever they may be found. Though most of the activities I specify to illustrate various points come from modern life, this is a matter of convenience for the author and presumably for many readers as well.

A LOOK AHEAD

The following is a brief overview of themes and some highlights of chapters to come. Chapter 2 presents the only extensive discussion of how other social thinkers and theorists regard solitary action, or, better put, how they disregard it. The chapter examines a broad range of social thinkers and theorists from Thomas Hobbes and Karl Marx to George Herbert Mead, Erving Goffman, and Harold Garfinkel.

Chapters 3–5 serve as the core chapters of the book by developing at length my conceptual account of solitary action. Though chapter 3 develops a frame of reference for analyzing the elements of solitary action, readers may be interested to note that before the abstract analysis begins I present two illustrative cases of the analysis of solitary action. The first involves the familiar game of solitaire, while the second involves the somewhat less familiar practices of performing solo jazz improvisations on the piano.

Chapter 4 develops a basic formula for the classification of four different forms of solitary action. Three of the four forms are discussed at length: peripatetics, regimens, and engrossments. The fourth form, reflexives, is more complex and receives a full account in chapter 5. Chapter 4 also includes a discussion of mental peripatetics, for example, daydreams, fantasies, and reminiscences, which I regard as socially structured activities that do not quite qualify as solitary actions.

Chapter 5 covers reflexives, which, broadly speaking, involve trains or chains of contextually reflexive cognitive or artistic development. A distinction is drawn between intuition and contextually reflexive solitary action. Attention is also devoted to the rare phenomenon of the epiphany and the uses of reflexive activity in solitary confinement.

Chapter 6 is an epilogue devoted to discussions of three forms of solitude. The chapter is an epilogue because solitudes, in my view, are relatively rare solitary conditions or events in which spiritual, aesthetic, or emotional experiences take priority over whatever solitary actions may be going on. Three quite distinct realms of solitude are discussed: the solitude of the religious vocation, the solitude of refined retreat, and the solitude of withdrawal in times of personal distress.

Chapter 2

Why the Invisibility of Solitary Action?

OVERVIEW

The British sociologist Colin Campbell (1996, pp. 4–5 passim) perceptively nominates the term "social action" as one of the most ubiquitous terms we use to define the subject matter of our discipline and one of the least examined terms as well. Why do we bother modifying "action" with the adjective "social?" If the two terms always appear together then the adjective "social" implies no distinction. It is, in effect, an invisible modifier widely used in a taken-for-granted way. Perhaps it is because of this taken-for-granted adjective that when I introduce the notion of solitary action many questioners often seem perplexed: Isn't it true that actors remain social when they are by themselves? Are we not a sociable species? If solitary action is as prevalent as you say, why have leaders in the study of action failed to notice it before now? My sense in listening to the tone of these comments is that sociologists are not only skeptical or perplexed by the notion of solitary action, but there seems to be some kind of intuitive sociological aversion to the image of an individual doing things while unaccompanied by others. Perhaps the term "social" tacitly shapes our understanding of action after all.

In this chapter I pursue one simple goal, to shed light upon prominent sources of this sociological aversion to regarding solitary action as a realm of a diverse set of behaviors no more or less of sociological interest than interaction or the subtle means by which strangers coordinate their behavior with one another in public places. Let me preface all other remarks by placing brackets around matters regarding exclusion or alienation as primary sources of the aversion to considering solitary action as a suitable phenomenon for sociological inquiry. The loneliness, depression, and sometimes the shame of those who are excluded or alienated from society is a part of social reality that social thinkers and humanitarians at large have always decried. But solitary action is not performed exclusively or even primarily by individuals who are stigmatized, ostracized, or disaffected. Solitary actions are interwoven in our everyday lives along with interaction and participation with others in small and large groups. These other forms of action have been studied extensively. How does it happen that solitary action has been ignored? It certainly can't be because all solitary action is inherently trivial. A fair number of the greatest artistic and intellectual achievements in Western civilization have been produced by men and women working in a place of their own, disengaged from whatever else may have been going on around them. But then untold numbers of people whose accomplishments are more modest work alone for some part of each day as well. There are also manifold types of solitary recreation and relaxation. Though many solitary activities are carried out in secluded settings, if we observe a busy street or a crowded shopping mall and simply filter out all forms of conduct where people are actively engaged with others, we will still find numerous instances of behavior to observe. Why do sociologists seldom notice what solitary individuals do or how they behave when a fair portion of all activities in the ordinary course of events are performed by individuals doing things on their own?

By their nature, these questions entail a degree of measured criticism of prevailing sociological theories of action. In the contemporary literature the best-known work along these lines is Colin Campbell's *The Myth of Social Action* (1996). Inspired by Max Weber's emphasis on the subjective meaning actors ascribe to their behavior, Campbell takes issue with the neglect of subjectivity in contemporary sociological and philosophical accounts of action, accounts that range from ordinary language philosophers to a broad and eclectic range of social theorists who address the notion of social action in numerous ways. Given this breadth, it is perhaps not too surprising that some of my critical remarks in this chapter converge or intersect with points advanced in Campbell's work. Such points of convergence are most notable in the latter portion of this chapter where discussion turns to the works of George Herbert Mead, Erving Goffman, and Harold Garfinkel. But it is of some importance for readers to keep in mind the differences between Campbell's critical themes and the purposes I pursue here. As I mentioned in chapter 1, I have nothing to gain by denying the reality of individuals who are subjectively conscious of their own actions and the meanings of their behavior in terms of their interaction and relationships with others. However, my criticisms here bear on a different issue. I am concerned with questions of why sociology in general has been averse to the study of solitary action and how theorists such as Mead, Goffman, and Garfinkel managed to avoid, and in some instances, diminish or dismiss this entire realm of behavior that is such a widespread feature of everyday life.

If we understand how it has happened that sociologists have managed to leave solitary action out of account, and if we realize that the reasons for these oversights are misleading or simply off the mark, then we will have cleared some intellectual ground to begin an analysis of solitary action. Ideally, like some sort of exegetical magician, it would be possible to locate one deep flaw running straight through the history of social thought, which, as if pulling a rabbit from a hat, would reveal the one great source for the oversights in our work. But I have no magic tricks to offer here. In reality, the neglect of solitary action develops in two quite disparate literatures. The first appears as a recurrent theme in classical or early modern social thought. The problem here begins with a philosophical overemphasis on the nature of the individual as a social animal. The second literature encompasses the intellectual programs of the three authors whose works on the sociology of action still shape how we think about the enactment of social conduct today, namely Mead, Goffman, and Garfinkel. Far from pulling an exegetical rabbit out of a hat to draw the oversights of these three together, each managed to avoid or sidestep solitary action in his own distinctive way. The only thing that can be said collectively about them is that in each case their aversion to solitary action is unconvincing or unnecessary.

SOCIAL ANIMALS AND THE ISOLATED INDIVIDUAL

Any list of classical social theorists with an aversion to entertaining thoughts about solitary action quite likely would begin with Emile Durkheim. After all, who among us has not read (and possibly taught) Durkheim's first chapter from *Rules of Sociological Method* ([895] 1982), in which he declares that virtually everything in social life begins as a collective social fact.

Durkheim was actually a more subtle thinker than his often overly programmatic chapter on social facts would suggest. Indeed, in his view ([1898] 1973) the moral organization of modern culture presupposes the liberties, dignity, and capacity for reason of the individual. Durkheim never extensively pursued the centrality of the individual in modern culture. But his brief allusion to the sacred space that surrounds the individual suggests a line of thought that might lead to some recognition of solitary undertakings, at least insofar as modern societies are concerned. Perhaps we might place some of the responsibility for the sociological aversion to solitary action at the door of Talcott Parsons. It is true that Parsons stressed action as a unit of analysis early in his career, and this might have been used to consider how individuals do things by themselves. Nevertheless, Parsons's problem of social order so dominated the mainstream of mid-century social theory that questions of social interaction that were beginning to be raised remained a specialty for mavericks for many years. It was Dennis Wrong ([1961] 1976, Ch. 1) who burst the Parsonian bubble with his iconoclastic critique of the over-socialized conception of man. Still, neither Parsons nor Wrong really put any roadblocks in front of the study of solitary action. They simply were concerned with other things. To identify the insights that made it difficult to consider solitary action in classical thought, we need to look elsewhere.

The deepest reason in classical social thought for skepticism regarding solitary action is the intense concern on the part of many thinkers to impress upon their readers that the human individual is a social being through and through. Indeed, there sometimes seems to be an undertone of anxiety in the way some authors make this point, as if to say anything at all about the individual apart from society would be a categorical mistake. One of the most forthright statements of this position appears in a passage from a discussion by Georg Simmel in which he supports the dyad as opposed to the isolated individual as the most basic unit of sociological analysis.

The mere fact that an individual does not interact with others is, of course, not a sociological fact, but neither does it express the whole idea of isolation. For, isolation insofar as it is important to the individual, refers by no means only to the absence of society. — On the contrary, . . . (i)solation attains its unequivocal, positive significance only as a society's effect at a distance—whether as lingering-on of past relations, as anticipation of future contacts, as nostalgia, or as an intentional turning away from society.[1]

Simmel's remarks, which are quite correct in themselves, are also, in effect, an exercise in rendering solitary action an invisible form of behavior. It is true that isolation can be socially defined by the circumstance that brought the individual to a state of being unaccompanied by others. Moreover, if the individual is isolated by virtue of some sort of voluntary or involuntary estrangement, that is all we may need to know, which would appear to be what Simmel means to suggest. But isolation may not imply estrangement at all. Isolation can also be a state that individuals seek out in order to do something

1. Simmel's remarks appear in a passage wherein he argues that all forms of solitude and isolation must be understood in the context of social relationships. Even moments of solitude enjoyed as part of ordinary life in a marriage are understood by Simmel as an element in the marital relationship. Hence, for Simmel, the question of what marital partners (or people in other situations) actually do when they are by themselves is obscured by the social relationship and never really arises as a question in its own right.

by themselves without interruptions that would be generated through contact with others. Moreover, we can distinguish different kinds of positive isolations in terms of the kind of activity the unaccompanied individual pursues. For example, there is a pronounced difference between what unaccompanied artists do in their studios and what unaccompanied anchorites do on religious retreats. We may still speak here of society's affect at a distance. The artist may paint in a culturally established genre. The anchorite may seek religious enlightenment according to a long-standing theological tradition. But these sought-after forms of isolation do not exclusively gain their positive significance from external social influences and relations as Simmel suggests. The condition of being alone is intrinsically defined by the kind of activity that is best performed while disengaged from others.

Simmel's remarks illustrate the anxious eagerness on the part of many sociologists to accentuate the social influences on the solitary actor. But what kinds of influences are at issue when we speak of society acting at a distance on even the most isolated individual? If we look back through the history of classical sociology to a passage from Karl Marx, and much further back to a surprising but quite significant comment by Thomas Hobbes, we find two different items, each of which stems in its own way from the philosophical proposition that the human condition is social rather than solitary.

Writing in *The Grundrisse*, Marx ([1859] 1973, p. 84) asserts in a passage that, though unpublished in his lifetime, is well known today:

> The human being is in the most literal sense a zoon politikon, not merely a gregarious animal, but an animal that can individuate itself only in the midst of society. Production by an

isolated individual outside society—a rare exception which may never well occur when a civilized person in whom the social forces are already dynamically present is cast by accident into the wilderness—is as much an absurdity as is the development of language without individuals living together and talking to each other.

Given that Marx conceived societies in terms of exploitative class relations and structural contradictions, this passage might seem out of place. However, Marx's thought moves here on a higher, more generalized, philosophical plane. The passage pivots on the description of the individual as a "zoon politikon." Though commonly taken to mean political animal, that meaning is correct but incomplete. The term originates in Aristotle's *Politics* (Book I, Ch. 2., 1252b, line 27–1253a, line 17), where he derives the notion of a state from the more basic notion of a shared community. Without going into exegetical detail, to say that the human individual is a zoon politikon is to suggest that he is a social no less than a political animal. This inherently social quality of the individual is the point that Marx wants to make in using the term here. Moreover, in a very brief space, Marx manages to cast the human being as a social animal in two distinct respects. In the first place the individual is gregarious or in other words inherently sociable. Hobbes, as we will see, makes the same point in a more ostensive way. In the second place, and with greater emphasis, Marx insists that the notion of an isolated individual is absurd. How so? Because whatever we do, be it material production or our use of language, we acquire the practices we employ as members of society. So the human species is social in that we are both sociable and socialized. Marx, in effect, gives us a more specific appreciation of two ways in which, as Simmel would say, even in the case of the isolated individual, society operates at a distance.

Thomas Hobbes might seem to be the least likely author in the history of social thought to conceive the human being as a social animal. And in most instances it is quite true that his thought begins with the notion famously articulated in *Leviathan* ([1651] 1968, p. 188) that in the absence of a dominating political authority, society would revert to a *bellum omnium contra omnes*, a war of all against all. But apparently Hobbes either received or anticipated that critics would find fault with a political philosophy that failed to take the human social condition into account. In a long and carefully crafted footnote at the very beginning of *De Cive*, Hobbes sought to put this criticism to rest. Anticipating Marx and Simmel despite the early date of his work, Hobbes ([1647] 1998, p. 24) is no less emphatic that the individual is a social animal from the start.

> Since we see men have in fact formed societies, that no one lives outside society, and that all men seek to meet and talk to each other, it may seem a piece of weird foolishness . . . [to insist] that man is not born fit for society. Something must be said in explanation. It is indeed true that perpetual solitude is hard for a man to bear by nature or as a man, i.e. as soon as he is born. For infants need the help of others to live, and adults to live well.

Note well that Hobbes not only casts the individual as a social animal, but he does so with reference to the same points that Marx would later raise. First, the individual is sociable or gregarious, seeking out the company of others, needing the help of others to live well, and finding perpetual solitude hard to bear. Second, albeit more implicitly than Marx, human beings are socialized animals relying on society to survive just as an infant needs others to care for her or him.[2] Implicitly, we need to acquire a full set of social practices from our society in order to survive.

But as with Simmel's insistence that society acts at a distance on even the most isolated individual, we may accept the two distinct ways in which Marx and Hobbes rightly portray the social nature of the human condition without thereby denying that we are individually or as a species capable of doing anything at all by ourselves. Though we might name some exceptions, very few human beings can comfortably and contentedly live for extended periods without any social contact with others. (I shall have more to say on forms of prolonged isolation in chapter 6.) It is no less true that we cannot survive on our own until we are fully socialized, that is to say until we have numerous social tools in our "toolkit," to borrow Ann Swidler's (1986) very useful phrase. But despite the fact that Marx and Hobbes contrast our social nature against the notion of the isolated individual, we can fully accept their insights and still acknowledge that humans can and do act on their own. Are we a gregarious species? Yes, but only to a certain extent. If we find prolonged solitude difficult to endure, we also find prolonged sociability difficult to sustain. It is not just that acting in concert with others involves effort and ultimately produces fatigue, though this is true in common experience. It is

2. Hobbes has to execute some fine theoretical turns to maintain his view of the social condition of the human species without contradicting his view of the harsh conditions of human relations in the absence of the supreme power of the state. His strategy in brief is to argue that by nature all individuals seek honor or advantage over others. Since this condition doesn't change with socialization, the war of every individual against every other is compatible with Hobbes's notion of the dependence of infants on others in order to survive. Nor does an inherent drive to compete deny the human urge to socialize with others. Sociality, after all, is a necessary condition for competition and the honor that results from success.

also that solitary activities have various attractions and appeals of their own. There are times when we gravitate to solitary activities even when we have options available to socialize with others. Moreover, and here we come back to the same point introduced when commenting on Simmel, we may indeed require socialization before we can do anything by ourselves. But it would be to present an over-socialized conception of the human condition, albeit not the same over-socialized condition that Dennis Wrong had in mind, to maintain that the skills and practices we acquire from society could only be employed when dealing with others. In other words, socialized individuals are quite capable of acting alone.

Exegetical criticism illuminates how the deep-seated and oft-repeated contrast between the human social condition and the isolated individual can so easily allow solitary action to silently slip through the sociological cracks. But the edifying effects of such exegetical criticism have their limits as well. It can be difficult to imagine specific cases from the abstract proposition that people sometimes gravitate to solitary activities. The easily accepted insistence that society acts upon us at a distance but that we can still do things on our own stands in need of substantive examples in order to envision solitary action on the ground. For these reasons I want to temporarily shift gears in what is mainly a theoretical chapter to offer an example of one kind of solitary action that has its own kind of appeal on the one hand and a plethora of solitary activities that in various ways illustrate society's influence at a distance on the other. The first comes from a small gem of sociological analysis of the calming effects of housework by the British sociologist, Bernice Martin. The second returns us to Daniel Defoe's *Robinson Crusoe* for a closer look at the influences on his solitary improvisations.

BEYOND SOCIABILITY: AN ILLUSTRATIVE
EXAMPLE FROM BERNICE MARTIN

As illustrated in the foregoing assertions by Marx and Hobbes, it is quite possible to overstate the case for human gregariousness or sociability. Just as every culture has its forms of sociability, so too every culture has its forms of solitary behavior. For example, in certain pre-modern cultures anxious or worried people methodically manipulated circular strands of beads by themselves, often using the beads in conjunction with silent or whispered chants or prayers. Though devout Roman Catholics may still use beads when saying prayers by themselves today, in most quarters of modern Western societies the use of beads to calm worries or other kinds of distress has largely disappeared. Indeed, the ebbing of religious practices in a secular age has left us with no commonly prescribed solitary rituals so that we may comfort ourselves and/or enable ourselves to feel as if we have some modicum of control within turbulent situations that are out of our hands. But even in the absence of rituals, people still find means of their own through commonplace forms of behavior to settle themselves down amidst the troubles in their lives. In a moment I shall turn to Bernice Martin for relevant insights in this regard, but it may be helpful to briefly underscore the larger theoretical issue involved here. It may sound plausible to the theoretically well-tuned ear to say that however social the human species may be in many respects, we are not instinctively or otherwise inclined to engage with others at every possible juncture as we make our way from one day to the next. But this highly general proposition begs all questions regarding what sorts of things we do by ourselves, how do we do them, and to what possible effect. Later on, in chapter 4, I shall develop a set of categories to classify different forms of solitary action that will provide a conceptual framework within which these questions can be addressed. But here and now the example from Martin may give readers a sense that it is more than an idle proposition to maintain that if we find it necessary or appealing to do things with others in some circumstances in our everyday lives, there are other circumstances when quite specific kinds of solitary activity can appeal to us as well.

In 1984, Bernice Martin, a British sociologist of culture and gender, and of relevance as well, a self-described (1984, p. 22) housewife of twenty years, published an article with the unusual subtitle, "Housework as Magic." Martin also composed the article in a curious way, making a case for housework as magic by tacking between themes in the poetry of W. H. Auden, studies in the sociology of gender, and personal reflections on her everyday life and the lives of those around her. Martin brings these sources together in support of a positive side of housework that is almost certainly more widely practiced than acknowledged or discussed. But what can possibly be "magical" about housework? Scrubbing floors and windows requires hard labor, preparing meals more often involves mindless routines than culinary ingenuity, picking up clutter and putting things back where they belong is a job that never ends. For the legions of women who perform these chores by themselves each day, these are also thankless tasks seldom even noticed by other members of the household. How can any of this be "magical?" Or, to put a more apt frame around the question: In what sorts of situations does housework become "magical"?

Martin (1984, p. 23) provides an answer to this question in the following reflection:

> My characteristic reaction to emotional turmoil is to clean the kitchen sink, scrub the work tops and tidy away the mess, of which there is always plenty cluttering the draining

board, sink, dresser, and so on; and then I cook—order first, then nurture.

This is a typical magic trick. Various emotional or family problems may be chronic and insoluble . . . but one can displace the locus of the chaos on to the kitchen mess, then there is solace and a kind of substitute solution in restoring order in the minor sphere which unlike the site of the real problem is genuinely under one's control.

For Martin then, and for a variety of other authors and acquaintances that she cites, the "magic" in housework is the sense of control it provides through the creation of household order. To be sure, this order is neither thorough on the one hand nor random on the other. Anyone who has tried to keep up with housework knows that a house is never immaculate. No matter how diligent and prolonged the effort, dirt lurks in out-of-reach places. An inspector general would find neglected fingerprints on the crockery and a towel somewhere that is not folded as smoothly as are all of its companions. The calming effect of housework lies not in creating perfect order, but rather in the activity of creating as much order as possible within a designated field. The author May Sarton,[3] who, like Martin, discusses the calming effects of household chores, provides an example in a passage from her *Journal of a Solitude* (1973, p. 109) of how this selective process works. Sarton, who throughout her journal chronicles a constant battle with neurotic emotions, set out one morning to cheer herself out of a spell of depression by cleaning out one of her household cupboards. But as she goes on to note, though the cupboard she

---

3. Martin does not cite Sarton. But the coincidence of their insights on housework substantiates Martin's claims.

chose was a mess, it was a viable mess compared to her paper cupboard which apparently was altogether too much to clean and organize in a morning's time. (For a more extended discussion of Sarton's periodic solitudes see chapter 6.)

Of special relevance here, the calming effects of housework set in when the housework is performed alone, which is to say, as a form of solitary action. Martin and Sarton both seek to create order in their material surroundings, which by some sort of "magic," in Martin's sense of the term, enables the individual to control her own feelings and thoughts. The importance of doing things by oneself as a means of creating some peace of mind is illustrated in a remarkable vignette included by Martin in her article.

According to Martin (1984, p. 20 passim), the order we need to create as a means to settle ourselves down is not only delimited but is symbolically significant to the individual as well. Martin tells the story of a good friend dying of cancer. All of her life this woman had strived to keep her house up to date and above all to meet the standards passed along by her mother for keeping one's bathroom clean. Now, though she had lost much of her strength, she was able to stave off reflecting on her own imminent mortality by continuing this one symbolically crucial practice. Cleaning a bathroom is neither easy nor pleasant for the healthy and strong and it must have been quite difficult for Martin's friend. But the relief to be gained from doing this chore, rather than others that might have been easier to manage, gave her comfort when she needed it most.

In the current context, notice that the calming effect of producing order through housework, the "magic" of which Martin writes, is best produced when the individual works by herself. It is, in its way, a quintessential instance of solitary action that too often goes overlooked. It is the actual production of order that provides the comfort and consolation, not the sheer fact that such order exists. Bernice Martin, no doubt, would have gladly cleaned her friend's bathroom, following every instruction down to the last detail. Or, arrangements might have been made for an experienced housekeeper to do the job. But her friend needed to do this work by herself and for herself. Notice this too: doing housework in emotionally turbulent situations may be a matter that takes priority over one's work on behalf of others. This comes through in a subtle way when Martin remarks in the passage excerpted above, "order first, then nurture." It is not a matter of neglecting wants and needs of others, but sometimes one must manage one's own problems first. This "magical" form of housework is solitary in a double sense: the individual is both the subject who performs the action and, reflexively, the person whose emotions are the object of the action as well.

THE WELL-SOCIALIZED IMPROVISER: ROBINSON CRUSOE

Earlier, when discussing Simmel, Marx, and Hobbes, I underscored the fact that we create an over-socialized account of the individual if we ignore the fact that insofar as action is concerned our socialization provides us with skills that allow us not only a degree of autonomy to behave in one way rather than another but also the capacity to innovate or improvise. This capacity is available to us in all kinds of actions, interactions, collaborations, and competitions. But solitary innovation or improvisation is particularly impressive. Here we see the influence of society at a distance, unshaped or refined by the collaborative contributions or the leadership, discipline, or enablements supplied by others. No matter how well socialized one may be, the individual is on their own. Of course, the degree to which such situations challenge the individual's abilities varies a great deal in different situations. Figuring out how to incorporate a few errant brush strokes in a painting may prove much easier than chasing down lost essential computer files when working alone on a critical deadline. But in either case, the influence of society at a distance only takes us so far. Beyond that point we must bring some ingenuity to the use of our socially acquired skills.

Though a moment of thought may bring to mind a collection of diverse forms of behavior where solitary individuals improvise or innovate based upon their ingenuity and their acquired skills, Defoe's fictional account of the pragmatic exploits of Robinson Crusoe illustrates solitary improvisation so well that, despite its origin in Defoe's imaginative fantasy, as a source of illustrations for solitary improvisations it seems suitable enough and impossible to resist.

The list of Crusoe's improvised accomplishments is remarkably long and Defoe describes some of his creative techniques in careful detail. The following list should provide sufficient indication of his practical ingenuity: Crusoe secured his tent with salvaged ship's rigging against a barrier wall he constructed from blocks of turf; later he constructed a beam for a tent; he produced basic tools including a pickax, shovel, and hod; later when his tools became dull he creatively improvised a foot-pedal-driven grinding wheel; he dug and braced a cave, rebuilt and improved it when it collapsed, and expanded it complete with a front door and later a back door as well; he created a workable lamp using tallow in a self-fashioned clay pot with salvaged cord for a wick; he made wicker baskets, discovering serviceable local substitutes for the sallow and willow branches ordinarily used; he produced pottery, a kind of ink, and even an umbrella, using local materials and imaginative techniques; he tailored his own clothing;

ultimately he even crafted a small boat. Crusoe apparently knew how to hunt when he arrived, and he had managed to salvage a rifle and powder that he used to kill game for food. Through trial and error he learned how to grow corn from salvaged seed. And he knew enough to be able to forage for local fruits, vegetables, building materials, and even tobacco (which he smoked in a clay pipe). He even captured a wild parrot, domesticated the bird, and began to teach it to speak. Crusoe also had a practical penchant for organizing his space and time. Time in particular mattered a great deal to him. As soon as possible after he arrived, he devised a crude calendar that enabled him to keep a journal and celebrate the Sabbath at regular intervals. He recorded climatic cycles that he used to determine the right seasons for various activities and then went on to develop a detailed seasonal division of labor. It would appear that he learned to determine the time of day as well, though his technique in this regard is not very clear.

To the extent that we allow ourselves to consider seriously the implications of Defoe's novel, Crusoe's remarkable array of improvisations obviously speaks against any suggestion that solitary action requires an over-socialized individual. To the contrary, it might seem more relevant to ask if he might be completely unsocialized: Did it matter that he was an early eighteenth-century Englishman of a certain social class, or were his clever ways of creating a life for himself on an inhospitable island the generic exercise of the pragmatic agency of a universal man? Based on a prominent passage early in the novel ([1719] 2003, p. 58) Defoe would have us believe that Crusoe relied on his "reason" alone, by which it would appear Defoe means what might otherwise be called his native intelligence or his "wits," rather than anything more grand that a philosopher of reason might have in mind. But one need not postulate an over-socialized individual to maintain that no matter how isolated an individual may be, he or she remains a member of a given culture with a certain way of life. It is sociologically interesting to regard Crusoe's solitary actions from this point of view.

In general it seems safe to say two things about the influence of culture on Crusoe's adaptations to his environment. First, most of his techniques for manufacturing things and for providing for himself with food are truly ad hoc improvisations that might be discovered through trial and error by a reasonably intelligent human being regardless of that individual's cultural origins. There are some exceptions. For example, Crusoe apparently knew the techniques of basket weaving from observations he made as a child and he learned how to make candles from sailors while at sea. But for basic techniques one needn't be a well-bred Englishman to dig out a cave, carve crude implements from stone and wood, and learn through trial and error how to successfully grow crops. In this sense, Robinson Crusoe demonstrates that creative and adaptive improvisation is a very real possibility when one works by oneself. But the second thing to say about Crusoe's actions brings culture back into play. English culture, or perhaps more broadly the culture of northwest Europe at the time, certainly left its mark on the ways of life and material habitat Crusoe produced, inhabited, and maintained. Crusoe's sense of time, for example, includes a Gregorian calendar complete with conventional English names for the seasons and months and some sense of conventional chronometry, at least to the point of hours as well. Then too, Crusoe may have come up with his own ways of making tools, but the tools he made resembled as closely as possible tools with which he was familiar. One must know how a grinding wheel driven by a foot pedal works to design one even if the final result is a jury-rigged contraption. Umbrellas, talking parrots, tobacco smoked from clay pipes: a solitary individual does not imagine such things out of the thin air. At one point Crusoe even envisions a design for his cave, complete with separate rooms for lodgings, a kitchen, and a dining room. Members of another culture might find a single great room acceptable, or perhaps a single division between lodging and a space to accommodate all other functions and activities. But, marooned though he was, Crusoe was still an Englishman and so was his solitary way of life.

SOLITARY ACTION AND THEORIES OF INTERACTION: THREE CASES OF NEGLECT

The preceding examples offer a glimpse into a rich order of social action. It may be counterintuitive to discover that in certain situations the dull rituals of housework may provide certain kinds of comfort in everyday life, just as Robinson Crusoe's practical ingenuity and clever cultural adaptations still captivate readers almost four hundred years after Defoe's novel first appeared. Solitary actions can be much more mundane. The examples here are meant to illustrate that there is a rich field of solitary behavior available for sociological inquiry and research. Indeed, the field of activities undertaken by individuals on their own is not only available to sociologists; it has barely been investigated at all. We encounter here a broad instance of sociological neglect.

One may excuse Hobbes and Marx for their imbalanced emphasis on the social characteristics of human behavior at the expense of activities performed by actors on their own. After all, as indicated above, they were philosophers, intent upon opposing philosophical perspectives in which every individual is conceived without regard to social influences of any kind. But we cannot so easily excuse the most influential twentieth-century sociologists of social interaction. Through their efforts, sociologists came to see the world of social interaction, a domain Erving Goffman

(1983) dubbed the interaction order, as filled with subtle and surprising maneuvers, complex processes of interpersonal coordination, and a multitude of extremely familiar practices that matter a great deal when we interact with others but that no one notices at all. Moreover, as the study of interaction moves into the twenty-first century, the three most influential first-generation scholars in the field, namely George Herbert Mead, Harold Garfinkel, and Erving Goffman, have directly inspired successive cohorts of scholars to pursue studies from within their personal perspectives and/or to carry their insights in new directions.[4] But this very influence has served to eclipse solitary action even more effectively than the philosophical antithesis proposed by Hobbes and Marx. It is a seldom-noticed yet remarkable fact that when we read Mead, Goffman, and Garfinkel we rarely catch sight of an individual doing something while disengaged from others. Robison Crusoe would be as out of place in Goffman's interaction order as he was on his deserted island. Bernice Martin would find little support for her insights into housework as "magic" either in Garfinkel's ethnomethodological studies or in the interactive processes conceptualized by Mead.

In order to open some legitimate space for the study of solitary action, it would help to know just why Mead, Goffman, and Garfinkel overlooked this entire domain. But there is no single answer. One might entertain the hypothesis that the over-socialized conception of the individual grew from early philosophical roots to become a pivotal postulate in sociology via the works of Durkheim and Parsons and then trace the influence of these over-socialized conceptions to the foundations of the study of social interaction.

4. Alfred Schutz must also be included as one of the founding fathers of the study of social interaction. But as matters stand in the second decade of the twenty-first century, Schutz no longer exercises anything like the degree of influence over current thinking as do Mead, Garfinkel, and Goffman.

But this hypothesis is untenable in several respects. First, though Garfinkel studied with Parsons, and Goffman had an obvious respect for elements of Durkheim's thought, neither of their respective bodies of work shows much evidence of adhering to a Durkheimian or Parsonian line. To the contrary, Garfinkel (1988, 2006), though expressing his respect for Parsons, distinguished his thought from Parsons's thought throughout his career. Mead, of course, wrote before Parsons and apparently had little or no acquaintance with Durkheim. Beyond this, since Mead, Goffman, and Garfinkel all found reason to stress the improvisational abilities of participants in interaction, the over-socialized conception of the individual in Dennis Wrong's sense of the term would not seem a problem for any of them. Instead, their notion of the individual may be overly sociable in the sense I introduced above. In order to see how or why these three independent and original thinkers found interaction so important but left solitary action in the dark, we must consider each author on his own.

George Herbert Mead

George Herbert Mead's social psychology has been rehearsed so many times that beyond a small circle of specialists his most influential ideas are now taken for granted. So much is this the case, that after we first encounter them, often in introductory texts, we may borrow them or cite them but rarely consider their implications. Thus it will hardly come as a surprise to find that Mead ([1924] 1964, p. 279) explicitly restricts his conception of a social act to "the class of acts which involve the cooperation of more than one individual." This exclusion is no accident. To the contrary, Mead's most well-known definition of social psychology—well-known because it appears in the opening pages of *Mind, Self, and Society* (1934, pp. 6–8)—describes a subject matter that makes sociality such a pervasive feature of social life that it would appear on this account that individuals never do anything by themselves at all.

> Social psychology studies the activity or behavior of the individual as it lies within the social process; the behavior of an individual can be understood only in terms of the behavior of the whole social group of which he is a member, since his individual acts are involved in larger social acts which go beyond himself and which implicate the other members of the group . . . we are starting out with a given social whole of complex group activity, into which we analyze [as elements] the behavior of each of the separate individuals composing it. We attempt, that is, to explain the conduct of the individual in terms of the organized conduct of the social group. . . . In social psychology we get at the process from the inside as well as the outside. Social psychology is behavioristic in the sense of starting off with an observable activity—the dynamic, on-going social process, and the social acts, which are its component elements. . . . But it is not behavioristic in the sense of ignoring the experience of the individual— the inner phase of the process or activity. On the contrary, it is particularly concerned with the rise of such experience within the process as a whole. It simply works from the outside to the inside (Mead, 1934, pp. 6–8).[5]

This programmatic summary of the subject matter of Mead's social psychology still sounds as bold and uncompromising today as it must have sounded to the students in the

---

5. The prolix style of this passage reflects the fact that like most publications, *Mind, Self, and Society* was composed via lecture notes recorded by his students.

lecture halls when Mead used this passage to open his lectures on mind, self, and society. Consistent with his definition of a social act as multi-party interaction, Mead conceives social life as a complex array of dynamic ongoing processes. For analytic purposes, we identify a specific social process and we may then identify social acts by situating them within these processes. Mead's most familiar social-psychological concepts today, the "I," the "me," and the "generalized other," all sit comfortably within this more expansive point of view. We assume from the start that an individual is engaged in a dynamic social process. There is no room here for disengaged activity. Some exterior circumstance or event generated within the process serves as a stimulus to act; the stimulus may provoke one or more spontaneous impulses to act (the "I") that the individual entertains as possible courses of action in light of how such actions may be regarded by others (the "me"), and/or in terms of the integration of the act into the larger ongoing process (the "generalized other").

Mead's enduring influence on the study of social action is almost certainly due to our intuitive sense that he grasps quite well some aspects of social life. Sociologists are well acquainted with processes that travel recursively via social interaction and joint acts through the minds and behavior of individuals and via their interactions with others flow back into the larger process as it goes on. Many different institutions and relationships may be analyzed in this way, from large-scale complex organizations and capitalist markets to nuclear families and intimate relationships. But intuitions, and especially intuitions that seem to have an undeniable ring of truth, sometimes make it easy to leave other aspects of social life out of account. Notice, from this point of view, Mead's definition of social acts exclusively in terms of interaction, and his interactive, processual view of life precludes any acknowledgment whatsoever of behavior conducted by individuals who by choice or circumstance find themselves disengaged from interaction. Daniel Defoe would find no way to tell us of Robinson Crusoe's technical ingenuity or cultural improvisations while marooned on a desert island from within the pervasively interactive theoretical world of George Herbert Mead.[6]

Does this matter? After all, Crusoe is only a fictional character. With extremely rare exceptions, people never face the challenges of self-sufficiency in difficult environments for any length of time. True enough: but people often do face what might be called Crusoean situations, circumstances where they must rely on their own ingenuity, skills, and imagination to solve a problem or find their way out of a predicament. Even in pre-modern times, where communal action was quite often the norm, shepherds still had to find lost sheep, solitary mariners had to keep leaky boats afloat, and messengers still had to make their way through unfamiliar or dangerous terrain. Having solved these problems on their own, they ultimately returned to village or tribal life. But they need not necessarily have publicized what they did. But if "Crusoean situations" are not hard to envision in pre-modern societies, it is all the more likely to find them in modern societies. Indeed, many occupations, from skilled blue-collar crafts to middle-level administration to most professions and so on, involve numerous and varied tasks where self-sufficient forms of behavior are intrinsic aspects of the job. Thus, plumbers and electricians are called upon to retrofit old infrastructure to

6. It is interesting to speculate on the different course that might have been taken by the sociology of action if the field had been inspired by Mead's close friend and fellow pragmatist John Dewey rather than Mead himself. Dewey (1922) had a less encompassing sense of interaction and was far more sensitive than Mead to the creative potential of solitary action. An indication of the lines of thought that open from a more Deweyan sense of action can be gleaned from Hans Joas's original and well-informed study, *The Creativity of Action* ([1995] 1996).

accommodate new needs, accountants are charged with balancing spreadsheets with imperfect data, and so on. It may be hard to imagine these modern individuals fabricating rudimentary tools or crude calendars on a desert island, but like Crusoe, they face challenges and predicaments themselves.

There are elements of Mead's thought such as his emphasis on culturally significant symbols in cognitive reasoning (intra-personal communication) that might seem to imply some sense of solitary action. But Mead's sweeping emphases on interactive social processes knits every thread of activity into the social fabric. Even a person's private reflections appear in Mead as an interaction within an ongoing social process. As we shall see momentarily, Mead's thoroughgoing interactionism eclipses more than just "Crusoean moments." But it is worthwhile first to consider the basic notion or principle that underlies Mead's encompassing sense of interaction. This notion is sociality, an idea that finds diverse expression in Mead's interactive concept of the social act, his dialogical sense of the interaction between the personal "you," the interpersonal "me," and the "generalized other," all mediated through communication via "significant symbols." What is sociality? In the interpretive literature, one can find two senses of the term. The first is the special sense of sociality that conceives the human species as a uniquely social animal by virtue of its unparalleled capacities for communication. There is a great deal to substantiate this sense of sociality as Mead's *idée maitresse*, given that he reacted against the individualistic psychological theories such as behaviorism that were widely disseminated during his time (cf. Joas [1980] 1985, p. 112. Ch. 5 passim). In a philosophical sense—and Mead after all was as much a philosopher as a social scientist—he appears to have felt a need similar to Hobbes and Marx to reject the idea of an entirely unsocialized individual. His solution was to postulate a pervasive communicative sociality as a defining characteristic of the species.

The sense of a fundamental idea of sociality in Mead is more speculative and hence less secure. Though Mead never managed to create a coherent philosophical system (Shalin, 2000, p. 314), according to an interpretation by David Miller (1973, pp. 23–25, Ch. 12), late in his life Mead introduced a broad notion of sociality that summarized his view of the most basic patterns of matter and life at large. In simple terms, this principle holds that all but the most confined elements in any given system simultaneously participate in one or more other systems as well. They are thus "social" in a philosophically abstract sense. Whether Mead held this all-encompassing view of sociality, and if so, whether he inferred it from his interactionist's view of social life or whether his view of social life was influenced by this expansive point of view, cannot be said with any certainty. However, at a minimum, Miller's interpretation suggests the degree to which a sense of sociality shapes and permeates Mead's point of view of social life. There is one more way to bring home the degree to which a sense of sociality pervaded Mead's thought. In a seldom-cited essay (transcribed lecture) included as an appendix to *Mind, Self, and Society* (1934 [1927], p. 385), Mead makes a virtue of sociality in terms that provide a down-to-earth intuitive sense of what sociality meant to him.

> All things worthwhile are shared experiences. Even when a person is by himself, he knows the experience he has in nature, [or] in the enjoyment of a book, experiences which we might think of as purely individual, would be greatly accentuated if they were shared with others.

There is something naïve in the scope of this last remark and something intellectually restrictive about conceiving social life at large in terms of sociality. This is not just a matter of "Crusoean moments." Consider the creation of household order that, as Bernice Martin suggests, can sometimes serve as a means to deflect and calm turbulent feelings. Would it necessarily be more worthwhile for the cancer victim, whom Martin describes, to share the chores of cleaning her bathroom with someone else? To the contrary, the creation of household order and its settling effects are produced in solitude, not interaction. Dealing with cancer and the waves of shock and panic that are its inevitable companions unquestionably makes for an extreme example. But at least in our individualistic modern cultures, there are moments when solitary activities, activities that do not necessarily sustain an ongoing social process, are more common than Mead's interactionist view of social acts might suggest. To take Mead's example, consider the varied pleasures of reading a book. Many people enjoy relaxing with a predictable plot and stock characters such as those found in police procedurals, detective stories, or romance tales. Some people ravenously read one volume after another of what is sometimes called formulaic fiction. Does it add to the relaxing experience of reading these novels to share the experience with someone else? Yes, at least for those who participate in book clubs devoted to such works; but no, for the large number of readers who read these novels for nothing more than the undemanding form of light entertainment they provide. Light reading is hardly the only popular form of solitary recreation that can be cited here. Indeed, puttering alone in the kitchen or basement, surfing peripatetically from item to item on the web or in newspapers or magazines are such common pastimes that we hardly notice them at all, and yet, it would certainly make a difference to the tenor of our modern everyday lives were we to be deprived of such forms of recreation for any substantial period of time.

One of the realities of modern life that Mead's all-encompassing sense of sociality and interaction obscures is how many situations leave us to find things to do by ourselves. The population of people who live by themselves has grown as young people form long-term relationships later in life and as divorce and separation have become familiar and accepted parts of the modern scene. Whether we welcome the freedoms of the single life or regret the difficulties in sustaining committed relationships, it would appear at the moment that the single life is a viable lifestyle replete with many forms of solitary action (cf. Klinenberg, 2012). As sociologists, we also need to account for the population of the elderly who live by themselves. Loneliness may be a serious problem for members of this group, especially for those who are incapacitated or find it difficult to connect with family or friends. However, a capacity for solitary action may be a singularly important coping mechanism here, as important in its own way for the elderly who live alone as Robinson Crusoe's technical ingenuity. Those who know how to invest themselves in solitary projects and how to organize their daily routines to suit themselves possess essential life skills.

Once we set aside the assumption of pervasive sociality, we can look beyond specific demographic groups and observe solitary actions in the most public settings of our daily lives. Consider the crowds riding public transportation during rush hours or scan the scene in bustling urban parks or suburban malls at noon. In such venues it would be hard to miss people engaged in single-player, high-tech games, watching videos on small laptop screens, browsing newspapers and magazines, carefully applying makeup, or finishing a bit of work they brought along from the office. And many of these folks may be multitasking as they consume foods and beverages specifically designed for the person on the go. It stretches a point to see these activities as social acts in

Mead's sense of the term. Yes, the information gleaned from the web or a magazine may find its way into conversation. But websites and magazine stories get read because they attract and hold the individual's attention, and no doubt, the majority of individuals involve themselves with a website or a story for their own personal interest rather than its value in conversation. Likewise, it may be possible to embed the office work done in the park or on a train into the flow of larger projects in a complex organization. We might even find a connection between the individual's work and some organizational form of the generalized other. But none of this does anything to obscure or deny the solitary qualities of the work processes performed by the individual on her own. Perhaps, like Crusoe, the solitary office worker may improvise solutions to work-related problems in a manner no one has ever had occasion to devise before, or she may take a shortcut or add improvements that the people who rely upon her work or authorize her assignment might not approve.

Given Mead's bent, it seems appropriate to bring discussion on his views to a close by posing a broad question in philosophical anthropology, that is, a question about the human species at large. We may infer from Mead's unqualified emphasis on sociality that in an ideal world humans would be disposed to gather, work, and play together continuously, or at least as much as would be practically possible in their everyday lives. Like all questions about human nature, there will never be consensus on an answer. However, it is worthwhile here to entertain a bit of negative evidence. In this case, the evidence comes from the Nazi concentration camps, perhaps the most extreme case in modern history of forcing large numbers of people into extremely small spaces. Of course the true horror of these camps was that the prisoners knew they were destined to be murdered, a shocking fact that must have induced panic and terror on the one hand and/or fatalistic resignation on the other. It is noteworthy then, that in his memoir of his time in the camps, Viktor Frankl, who would become a leading psychological theorist, found it worthwhile to mention the deep impression he took away from the effects of simply being forced to live in such closely crowded conditions:

> There were times when it was possible and even necessary, to keep away from the crowd. It is well known that an enforced community life, in which attention is paid to everything one does at all times, may result in an irresistible urge to get away, at least for a short while. The prisoner craved to be alone with himself and his thoughts. He yearned for privacy and for solitude (Frankl, 1984, p. 61).

Frankl's experience is unique, of course. Yet it does suggest that when human beings find themselves in close proximity, at some point the need to be alone—to avoid the scrutiny and continuous engagement becomes overwhelming. Just where we draw this line in everyday life rather than in the intolerable conditions of the concentration camp is a subject that would repay sociological investigation. But Frankl's reaction suggests that there may be limits to how much sociality individuals will bear willingly. And perhaps it may not be universally the case that sharing always enhances what we do by ourselves.

Erving Goffman: The Limits of the Interaction Order

Mead, Goffman, and Garfinkel are quite rightly grouped together as founders of the study of social interaction. But each of them created and inhabited his own intellectual world. With Goffman and Garfinkel we enter a world in which pivotal abstract principles like sociality no longer matter. Goffman in particular composed his work in an unsystematic and in certain respects undisciplined way. He hops from rich metaphors of interaction rituals among unacquainted individuals in public places to keenly observed descriptions of the gestures people perform to indicate they are together to social interaction in total institutions. Only late in his life, when he apparently knew he had developed a fatal disease, did Goffman summarize his subject matter in an essay entitled "The Interaction Order," delivered just before he died (by a reader on his behalf) as his Presidential Address to the American Sociological Association. For present purposes it is a matter of some interest to note that in that essay, even before Goffman begins to define the nature and substance of the behavior he includes within the domain he calls his own, he does his best to stake out boundaries of the field that include as much social interaction as possible. He reserves only a small margin for private, isolated behavior.

It is a fact of our condition that, for most of us, our daily life is spent in the immediate presence of others; in other words, whatever they are, our doings are likely to be, in the narrow sense, socially situated. So much so that activities pursued in utter privacy can easily come to be characterized by this special condition (Goffman, 1983, p. 2).

For those accustomed to Goffman's carefully crafted qualifications that usually buffer his broad generalizations,[7] the bright line he draws within the human condition between socially situated behavior, which Goffman claims as the human norm, and utterly private conduct, which he maintains is a rare and special condition, may seem quite blunt. It is not, however, as blunt as it

7. For a discussion of Goffman's undisciplined ways see an article I co-authored with Mary Rogers (Cohen and Rogers, 1994).

seems. By dividing all human behavior into two categories, one socially situated and the other utterly private, Goffman apparently means to include on the socially situated side all forms of behavior where human beings share the same space, or, to use one of Goffman's most useful tropes, all situations where individuals are co-present. By co-presence Goffman (1963, p. 17) means circumstances where individuals are in close enough proximity to perceive others and to be perceived by them.

Goffman engages here in a bit of analytical prestidigitation that makes many forms of solitary action disappear. What is wrong with his assertion? If all he means in saying that most social conduct happens in the company of others who have the opportunity, if they so choose, to mutually monitor one another's conduct, then in most cultures he may be more right than wrong. Although had Goffman been writing today, he might be surprised by the sizable population of people who live by themselves. Presumably, Goffman meant to exclude those who led more traditional forms of hermetic existence whose work isolated them from others for considerable periods of time, such as shepherds, cowboys, lighthouse keepers, night watchmen, and long-distance truckers. But while Goffman is not mistaken, his sense of co-presence as a normal state of affairs for the human condition is so broad that it makes it appear as if everyone within the presence of others is ipso facto engaged in some kind of interactive conduct. Goffman thereby fails to allow that actors may be in the company of others and tacitly sensitive enough to their surroundings to notice any unusual events (social disruptions or other kinds of environmental disturbances as the case may be), yet these individuals may still focus their attention on solitary doings of their own. Public behavior in library reading rooms provides a common and familiar case in point. A busy reading room may seat twenty or thirty patrons simultaneously, each within several feet of one another. Yet each individual may be privately involved in an activity on her own, almost fully engrossed in reading matter on a different subject. Why should we be interested in the relatively small amount of attention these individuals pay to one another when this is not their primary activity?

Goffman's inversion of the social and the solitary is not confined to an implication of a keystone remark in a programmatic summary of the field he claimed for himself. To the contrary, this inversion turns up periodically in his work as a kind of "sociological alchemy," a term Goffman (1974, p. 5) used to refer to "the transmutation of any patch of ordinary social life into an illuminating publication." Consider Goffman's account of civil inattention, which is highly regarded as a particularly subtle example of his acute sensitivity to interpersonal relations. According to Goffman (1963, p. 84), civil inattention requires anonymous actors to do nothing more than reciprocally acknowledge one another's presence and stay alert so that they neither intrude upon others, nor allow themselves to be intruded upon except insofar as practical conditions may require. Is civil inattention a form of interpersonal conduct? Yes indeed, as far as it goes. But even the term "civil inattention" itself suggests that the activity is sufficiently undemanding to allow a person to engage in all sorts of other things. Is the person standing silently next to you in an elevator chamber simply staring at the numerals announcing each floor; or is she rehearsing the items she is about to discuss at a meeting, deciding which numbers to pick for the lottery ticket she is about to buy, or preparing a mental list of things to pick up at the store after work? These are not matters of civil inattention but rather the things that actually may hold the majority of the attention of the individuals sharing the ride. Goffman (1963, pp. 38–42) performs a similar inversion in his account of "involvement shields." Involvement shields are objects or gestures that an individual manipulates so as to avoid an unwanted form of interpersonal contact. Involvement shields may be used to avoid unwelcome encounters or awkward interactions. But here again, Goffman in this case explicitly (1963, p. 38) asks us to direct attention to the socially situated aspect of the behavior and bypass the question of what the individual may be doing by herself. Yet we may be quite interested to know what kind of solitary activity is going on. Given Goffman's penchant for dramaturgical themes, it may be appropriate here to cite as an example a staple of certain scenes in spy thrillers. In such scenes, a character uses involvement shields (e.g., raising a page of a broadsheet newspaper to mask an act of surveillance or to cover a weapon as it is being raised). Here, in a dramatic fashion, the weakness of Goffman's strategy for transmuting a secondary aspect of conduct into the primary topic of interest comes to light. Should we notice the means of subterfuge or the activity that it conceals?

There is a sense in which drawing attention to how Goffman avoids acknowledging solitary action is like noticing how dramatists who write comedies avoid the tragedy in their plots (or vice versa). Goffman was blessed with a unique gift for bringing to light half-hidden evanescent facets of public behavior, and he did so with an inimitable ring of sociological truth. No one can doubt that the sociology of everyday life would never have come into its own in the last half of the twentieth century without him. But there is a downside to the awe he inspires insofar as the sheer brilliance of his writings can blind us to what he leaves out of account. There was a touch of what amounts to methodological exaggeration when he began his broad account of the interaction order by informing us that it is characteristic of the human condition that most behavior is socially situated. As a methodological device, the exaggeration served him well inasmuch as it allowed him to cast a sociological eye well beyond focused inter-action per se. Yet, whatever advantages Goffman gained by look-ing at the human condition in this way, his overstatement need not be accepted as an unchallengeable truth. In reality, there is behavior beyond the boundaries that Goffman staked out for the interaction order and we are free to look and see what we might find there.

Harold Garfinkel: Does Ethnomethodology Need to Exclude Solitary Action?

Harold Garfinkel never published a programmatic statement excluding solitary actions from the ambit of his ethnomethod-ological concerns. Unlike Mead, he was not a systematic thinker and hence he had no need to postulate sociality as a pivotal prin-ciple in his thought. Unlike Goffman, Garfinkel did not stake out a subject matter by conceiving as much human behavior as possible in terms of socially situated public activity. There are even moments in Garfinkel's more recently published works, as I shall indicate below, where the behavior Garfinkel studies need not involve any interaction at all. But these studies are rare exceptions during the course of his work. Even more than Goffman—the sociologist of everyday life he is most often com-pared to—Garfinkel devoted the majority of his investigations to face-to-face reciprocal interaction.[8]

Just why Garfinkel kept ethnomethodology's lens focused on interaction is difficult to say. One possibility might be that Garfinkel's commitment to systematic empirical demonstrations

8. This is especially the case for his most influential empirical studies, including his well-known "Experiments in Trust" (1963) and the empirical chapters in *Studies in Ethnomethodology* (1967).

of his ideas, a commitment that ran far deeper than it did in Mead or Goffman, disposed him to study interactive processes that could be readily recorded and analyzed in detail after the fact. But Garfinkel seems to have been driven to develop his uncommonly original insights much more than he was driven by his empirical commitments. So it seems likely that his emphasis on interaction and relative neglect of solitary action originates in these insights themselves.

Garfinkel's lasting importance as a theorist of action stems from two points that are so closely related in his approach that their distinction is only a matter of expository convenience. In the first place, Garfinkel conceives social conduct as constituted in the enactment of social practices. The familiarity of this notion today (e.g., in works by notables such as Giddens, Bourdieu, and Habermas, among others) should not be allowed to obscure how radically different it was from all other accounts of action during the period after World War II when Garfinkel began his work. Second, each move enacted during interaction is significant by virtue of its contextual reflexivity. What does contextual reflexivity mean? It means on the one hand that any move in an action makes sense only in terms of the context that has been developed through the moves that preceded it. Hence, if someone asks me: "Who was that at the party last night?" and I reply: "Maria, Elizabeth, Juan, and the rest of the bunch," the phrase "the rest of the bunch" makes specific sense only in that context. My interlocutor now asks: "Did Paul come with Maria?" This question not only makes sense in terms of the context of last night's party, but also in terms of the background knowledge we share about the partygoers. But notice that each move not only makes sense in terms of what came before, each move reflexively also advances the next context. For instance, asking about Paul and Maria moves the context to a specific situation in which these two people are somehow involved. So contextual reflexivity draws its significance from the preceding context and makes a contribution to context formation as well.

As will become evident in chapters 3–5, contextual reflexivity figures prominently in my analysis of solitary action. Despite Garfinkel's preference to study contextual reflexivity in interaction, it may be helpful here to have in mind a simple example of reflexivity in solitary action. Imagine a painter standing in her studio before a canvas on an easel. On the canvas she has painted a shadowy hill and a twilight sky. Now our painter adds a clustered flock of sheep moving along the top of the hill. This move by the painter makes a certain sense in this context. It makes sense that sheep cluster at twilight. Next the painter adds the figure of a shepherd, staff in hand, accompanying the sheep. The shepherd makes sense in terms of the sheep and simultaneously adds something new to the context. Notice the solitary quality of this small bit of reflexive context formation. The painter begins with a blank canvas, paints the shadowy hill, then paints the twilight sky, proceeds to add the flock of sheep, and then the shepherd. The context grows reflexively, each move taking its lead from the context previously at hand and then changing the context as well. But the painter makes each move by herself. No one else adds anything at all. She builds the context alone. Each move makes sense to her in context, and she alone comprehends how each addition moves the context along.

A few examples of solitary action come to light late in Garfinkel's career in a volume of previously unpublished studies compiled by Anne Warfield Rawls. For example, Garfinkel (2002, pp. 153–162) investigates how it happens that an individual recognizes the ring of her own phone versus rings that do not call for attention. Garfinkel (2002, Ch. 6) also investigates how actors follow written instructions, for example, for assembling a piece of furniture from a kit. Contextual reflexivity here often takes the form of trial and error. But it suffices to note that such assembly processes are often solitary ventures in which individuals puzzle out by themselves how things are supposed to work. But these late additions to Garfinkel's work are exceptions to his far more prominent studies in interaction. So we return to the question of why Garfinkel confined himself so often to studies of interaction.

A plausible reason for Garfinkel's preference for the study of interaction may be his aversion to the analysis of any and all processes taking place in the human mind. There is evidence from an expository essay Garfinkel composed as a graduate student (2006) that he earnestly opposed the conceptual analysis of subjective points of view, a line of thought identifiable in the works of Talcott Parsons, whose seminars Garfinkel was attending at the time. The young Garfinkel also appears disinclined to Husserlian questions of the ultimate foundations of thought. Be this as it may, by the time Garfinkel published his foundational works in ethnomethodology his aversion to the study of mental phenomena had become a programmatic, a priori announcement with a somewhat ghoulish metaphor (Garfinkel, 1963, p. 190):

> I shall exercise a theorist's preference and say that meaningful events are entirely and exclusively events in a person's behavioral environment. . . . Hence, there is no reason to look under the skull since nothing is to be found there but brains. The "skin" of the person will be left intact.[9]

---

9. Garfinkel is not alone in using macabre imagery to discount the body as the home of consciousness. Erving Goffman (1974, pp. 575–576) closes *Frame Analysis* with a lengthy quote from Maurice Merleau-Ponty who claims, inter alia, that behind an actor's face is "only darkness crammed with organs."

Whatever else may be said about Garfinkel's radical exclusions of subjective consciousness, it certainly did not make his project to develop a theory of action very easy. His "theorist's preference" is not to deny the existence of subjectivity but rather to set it aside and to leave it out of his accounts. He took a different path by stressing what Anne Warfield Rawls (in Garfinkel 2006, p. 60) calls the "objectivity of subjectivity." In simple terms, this phrase refers to the fact that during the course of social interaction one party will indicate a subjective state by various contextually reflexive behavioral moves. For example, if I am subjectively impressed by how knowledgeable someone seems to be about a topic under discussion, I may exhibit this mental impression in a behavioral move by asking the individual to tell me more about what she or he knows. Now, the point is not simply that I have expressed my mental respect in public, but that I have made it available to be recognized by the other party. Thus, my mental impression becomes real (objective), insofar as it is acknowledged by the other party who might respond, for example: "I'm not as well-versed in the matter as you may think."

Garfinkel introduces this way of dealing with mental states during the course of at least two articles in *Studies in Ethnomethodology* (1967, pp. 56, 256–270). But in both instances he acknowledges that by concentrating only on the side of mental life that the actor makes publicly available in interaction, he leaves out of account whatever aspect of mental life the actor may withhold. Moreover, Garfinkel goes on to assume that the actor maintains the capacity of autonomous control, an assumption that arguably overstates the case.[10] However this may be, by

---

10. Blushing is a quite vivid example. Other examples may be talking more or less than others; telling slips of the tongue; changes in register, cadence, or tone of voice.

allowing the operations of the mind into the sociology of action only through behavior that exhibits subjectivity only as it is acknowledged by others, Garfinkel makes it impossible to consider the reality of solitary action. Consider the simple example of a shepherd guiding a flock of sheep out to a pasture. Through experience our shepherd has learned that if the sheep at the front of the flock move too fast, those at the rear will become stragglers and may get lost. Therefore, she monitors the pace of the leaders and slows them down when necessary. No one is there to see her put her knowledge to use. But does this make her knowledgeable action any less real? Perhaps some day she will have occasion to pass along her knowledge about how to manage sheep. Then, of course, Garfinkel might step in and analyze how she instructs her apprentice. But the shepherd may have been managing sheep for many years before that day arrives. And she has kept the sheep moving time after time. Though this solitary action among a myriad of others seems beyond the reach of Garfinkel's studies in ethnomethodology, it is undeniably a basic part of everyday life.

In many respects, I believe Garfinkel's extraordinarily original insights into human conduct were facilitated by his willingness to shift sociological attention away from mental states and toward the enactment of behavioral processes. As will be evident in the next chapter, I have benefited a great deal from his insights in my own views on solitary action. Nevertheless, in placing radical brackets around all forms of mental life that remain unacknowledged in social interaction, Garfinkel makes it almost impossible to conceive certain dimensions of the activities individuals carry on by themselves. Even Goffman (1967, pp. 2–3), who also focused his attention on how activities are performed, acknowledged the need for a minimal psychology of the acting individual sufficient to allow him to flesh out behavioral processes in a realistic way. Had Garfinkel made the same small allowance, perhaps solitary actions might have figured more prominently in his work.

CLOSING REMARKS

The raison d'être of the sociology of action is to discover aspects of human behavior that we take for granted to the point they don't seem to be there at all. There is a peculiar sense in which this is true for solitary action. It is true that all of us do things by ourselves each day without noticing what we are doing at all—we brush our teeth, tie our shoes, walk down the hall, turn on the lights, and so on. But it is also true during the course of our everyday lives that we do things that fix our attention—we read a book, improvise a repair for a household item, or study for exams. For some people, solitary action constitutes part of their occupations or careers, for example, artists and practitioners of skilled crafts work by themselves. Indeed, I am by myself as I write these words, and writing itself is such a focused kind of action that I could hardly be unaware of what I am doing. The people who seldom notice solitary action are those who established the field in which we study social action today.

An odd aspect of the virtual neglect of solitary action by Mead, Goffman, and Garfinkel is that they each had their own ways of setting the solitary domain aside: Mead left no room for solitary action in his system of thought, Goffman confined himself to the public side of disengaged behavior, and Garfinkel ruled out mental activity by fiat. Perhaps a historian of social thought will someday propose implicit lines of continuity between their oversights, and perhaps a particularly bold historian will tie the omissions of twentieth-century theorists of action to the preference for sociability that we find in classical social thought. But then perhaps there is no single reason to be found. After all, Marx, Durkheim, and Weber each laid the groundwork for the sociology of modernity without completing a conceptual account of the modern state. But there appears no single reason for their neglect.

In any event, my purposes in this chapter have been ostensive, not historical. The fact is that in sociology we have yet to recognize that there is more to what members of society do each day than what they do in the company of others. None of us may ever find ourselves marooned in the manner of Robinson Crusoe, but most of us have had our share of Crusoean moments in our lives. And many of us have known the "magic" of putting things in order by ourselves, whether it is a bathroom, a kitchen, a closet, the basement, or our desks. How shall we conceive of solitary action? What are its elements and its various substantive forms? These are the questions I shall now proceed to address.

Chapter 3

The Elements of Solitary Action

How do we do things on our own? In this chapter I develop an analysis of the elements of solitary action to answer this question. As readers will see, this question is really a variant of the well-established question: What is social action? This is a topic others have addressed with primary concern for how people interact and produce action together. My answer, though addressed to solitary action, will borrow and reorient useful elements from theorists of interaction, including Garfinkel, Mead, and Goffman, covered in my critical discussion in chapter 2.

Throughout the present chapter I try to temper my concern for the second-order analysis of the elements of solitary conduct with examples that keep the discussion tethered within sight of the richer realities of conduct as carried out in everyday life. One strategy I employ to this end is to thread two extended examples through much of the discussion. My first example is the way the humble game of solitaire is played. Even before Microsoft made solitaire the most popular diversion for computer users around the globe, it already was played perhaps millions of times each day, almost always by one player alone. My second example is playing solo jazz improvisations, a much less common activity, brilliantly analyzed by David Sudnow in *Ways of the Hand*, a book that, perhaps unwittingly on Sudnow's part, brought ethnomethodological insights across the boundary from interaction into the solitary realm.[1] Here I present a close look at the play of each of these activities highlighting analytical aspects of behavior that I will distinguish and discuss conceptually thereafter. These examples then anticipate as well as illustrate some of the major themes in the chapter. But the relevance of these examples extends beyond my immediate concerns. Chapters 4 and 5 present extended discussions of categories of solitary action. Unlike the analytical elements of solitary action discussed below, these categories distinguish types of solitary action that occur in various settings in everyday life. The game of solitaire and the solitary development of jazz improvisation each exemplify a category in this more substantive scheme. Solitaire is an instance of the category I call engrossments (see chapter 4). Jazz improvisation is an example of the category I term reflexives (see chapter 5).

SOLITARY BEHAVIOR: TWO EXAMPLES

Solitaire

By its very name, solitaire declares itself a game played by one.[2] Though easily dismissed as a trivial pursuit, it serves to preoccupy its players' minds, a trait that makes solitaire a commonly used buffer for the worried, a tranquilizer for the anxious (discussed in chapter 2), a comfort for the distraught (similar in this

1. I have also consulted Robert R. Faulkner and Howard S. Becker's sociological analysis of jazz musicianship, *Do you Know . . . ? The Jazz Repertoire in Action*, and have drawn from their autobiographical reflections on their development and part-time careers as professional musicians.

2. Though all forms of solitaire can be described in broadly similar terms, I will refer here to Yukon, which is the game's most familiar variant. This is one of the two forms of solitaire available on the current editions of Microsoft Windows operating systems. However, for present purposes it does not matter whether the game is played with a computer, a hand-held electronic device, or on a table with a physical deck of cards.

sense to the "magic" of housework), an enabler for procrastinators, and an escape for the bored. Though the play of the game is about as uncomplicated as a card game ever gets, its effects can be quite remarkable. Indeed, many players become so caught up in the turn-by-turn play that they do not bother to keep a running score, and even more remarkably, they often continue to deal new cards even after they complete numerous perfect hands.

The key to solitaire's preoccupying effects lies in its elementary moves. Each deal of the cards in solitaire forms a self-contained starting point from which the player unfolds a context according to a small number of formulaic rules.[3] But, simple though it is, the solitaire player's context formation shares the elementary features that ethnomethodologists have discovered in the complexities of interpersonal conversation. Just as a conversation unfolds as each turn of talk makes sense in terms of what has been said before and reflexively reinstates or alters the context in which the next speaker's turn will make sense, so too in solitaire each move in the game makes sense in terms of the previously developed pattern of cards on the table (often called the tableau in written descriptions of the game) and reflexively, each move alters the contextual pattern of the tableau for the next move.

This contextual reflexivity becomes clear in the details of how moves are made in the game. A contextual tableau is created at the beginning of a game by arranging a series of seven stacks of cards in a graduated order (i.e., the first stack has one card, the second stack has two cards, and so on), with the top card in each stack face up and the rest face down. In addition, the tableau includes space for the player to create four piles by placing available cards from the same suit in descending order from ace to deuce. The object of the

---

3. For an excellent study of rules and constraints during the play of interpersonal games see DiCicco-Bloom, B. and Gibson, D.R. (2010).

game is to build four same-suit piles in these spaces. At the start of the game the player moves any available aces from the face-up cards into the open spaces and also makes matches on the face-up cards in the seven stacks. These matches proceed by alternating suits.

So how does contextual reflexivity operate here? Even in the opening moves the player reflexively scans the face-up cards for matches and then makes the matches that are found by moving cards to appropriate piles or stacks, which has the effect of changing the context in the tableau. After all initial matches have been made, context formation proceeds by drawing three cards from the deck, with the third card available for new matches. When new matches are made, a new card becomes available from the three that have been drawn. When cards are matched by movements from the seven stacks, other new cards are revealed. Each match made and each new three-card draw constitutes a reflexive move as the context continues to unfold. When no new matches can be made, context formation comes to an end. If all cards have been moved to the ace-to-deuce same-suit piles, the player wins. If, however, the ace-to-deuce same-suit piles are incomplete, the player loses. In either case, the cards can be shuffled, a new hand dealt, and the context formation process begins once again.

Though context formation starts over with each deal of the deck, two traits of solitary activity are notable here. First, despite its simplicity, the game requires certain cognitive skills. Cards must be matched in very specific ways and piles must be built in the prescribed ace-to-deuce sequence. Since the context changes with every move, the player must exercise vigilance so as not to overlook an available match. A player who fails to make an available match precipitously reduces her chances to win. Second, solitaire is a game that engages the player in building context in a simple powerful rhythm. The initial tableau is dealt and scanned, cards are moved, matches are made; then three new cards are drawn, the tableau is scanned, cards are moved, matches are made; then a new draw is made; scan, move, match, and draw; scan, move, match, and draw again until no more matches and moves can be made. This is of course not the only rhythm of solitary behavior. Nor are all forms of solitary behavior rhythmic at all. But like the rhythms of repetitive physical exercise and silently repeated prayers, such rhythms enable certain kinds of solitary activity to produce hypnotic effects. And it can be suggested that this rhythmically induced trance provides solitaire with some of its unusually effective power to suppress anxieties, blunt psychic pain, and defer engagement in onerous tasks.

Jazz Improvisation

My second example of solitary behavior, performing jazz improvisations on the piano, seems so different from playing solitaire that few instructive similarities initially come to mind. These differences should not be underestimated. While solitaire offers virtually no room for variation in the moves players make, jazz improvisation offers numerous possibilities for players to generate unique, complex variations of their own. While each hand of solitaire is self-contained, leaving no contextual development for the next deal, jazz musicians often improvise a string of distinct variations on a single song or brief musical phrase. Solo improvisations on a given melody carry over from session to session, sometimes continuing throughout the course of a musician's career.[4] Then too, while solitaire is rarely part of a larger, ongoing social process, jazz improvisation must be learned, and often, at least some (though rarely all) of that learning involves interactive

---

4. For examples and discussion of the jazz repertoire see Faulkner and Becker (2009).

instruction or face-to-face encounters with experienced musicians. The mature improviser also will almost certainly collaborate with others at least part of the time. Even one-of-a-kind featured improvisers like Thelonious Monk alternated solos and background work with other members of a combo or band.

Yet jazz improvisation is not entirely a world apart from solitaire, and the similarities can be instructive for understanding solitary action. To begin with, the inherent sociality of some aspects of jazz musicianship notwithstanding, some of the most essential skills and basic elements in a jazz player's repertoire are commonly acquired and developed by the player when he engages with the music by himself.[5] Learning basic skills is one such example. No matter how often a musician takes lessons, the necessary practice sessions between classes will be performed alone. For example, David Sudnow (1981, p. 33) reports that for many months during his early training he practiced by himself all day, every day. From their earliest days and throughout their playing careers, jazz musicians are on the lookout for interesting tunes to acquire for their repertoire. Musicians acquire some tunes through listening and playing with others. However, as Robert Faulkner and Howard Becker report, building a repertoire is also often a solitary affair. For example, Faulkner and Becker (2009, pp. 48–49 passim), each a part-time jazz performer as well as full-time sociologist, report learning some of their first tunes as young teenagers while listening to radio broadcasts or electronic recordings late at night in the darkness of their rooms. Part of what they learned was the skill to hear a tune and translate the music into playable notes. And this

5. Though I stress solitary activities in preparation for performance here, numerous jazz notables have recorded solo albums as well. The list includes Bill Evans (*Alone*), Bud Powell (*The Genius of Bud Powell*), Sonny Rollins (*The Solo Album*), Thelonious Monk (*Monk Alone*), Art Tatum (*Art Tatum: 20th Century Piano Genius*). The fact that pianists dominate the list (although Rollins is an exception) is almost certainly due to the piano's unsurpassed range of musical possibilities.

skill, in turn, enabled them to acquire new tunes quickly once they matured, quite often by listening repeatedly to recordings from their personal collections (2009, pp. 25–26 passim). Jazz improvisation relies on a stock of previously prepared material and a set of well-mastered skills. There will be more to say about these skills momentarily. However, the notable point here is that improvisers conduct a good deal of musical activity by themselves, preparing material that they weave into improvisations on the stand and honing skills they need to improvise by using this material in original ways when they perform.

It is a matter of only small significance in itself that jazz improvisers, like solitaire players, do things by themselves. But several features of improvisational performance technique can bear comparisons with solitaire so as to highlight generic, albeit highly variable qualities of solitary action at large. To this end I rely upon David Sudnow's finely grained analysis of how he mastered the basic skills of the improviser's craft. Though his account moves through developmental stages, in the end Sudnow (1981, p. 173) asks us to read his work as an elaborated definition of how jazz improvisation is played. But this is no casual description such as a music journalist might submit. Sudnow developed his insights during a period in which he studied and worked with Harold Garfinkel and Harvey Sacks,[6] who were, respectively, the founder and a leading light in the formation of ethnomethodology, which, more than any other sociological orientation to action is primarily attuned to the tacit procedures through which action is performed. Sudnow employs none of the conceptual ethnomethodological lexicon, nor, because he deals mainly with solitary action, does his study resemble a typical ethnomethodological analysis of interaction. Nonetheless, the

6. Sudnow's book is dedicated to Sacks, who died an untimely death in 1973.

ethnomethodologically well-versed reader will not find it too difficult to spot the intellectual underpinnings of Sudnow's understanding of improvisational jazz technique.

This is especially true with regard to contextual reflexivity, which, as noted above with regard to solitaire, is the turn-by-turn or move-by-move procedure through which each move only makes sense in terms of the context that previously has been produced, and, reflexively, each move makes a difference to the unfolding context of subsequent moves. The surface sound of jazz improvisation is easily described: the player performs a tune in a straightforward way and then proceeds to a series of alterations of elements of the theme, some of which may sound quite different from the theme itself. But this description does not deal with the inner reflexivity of the improviser's craft. To grasp what is going on in improvisation as an activity, it helps to begin, as Sudnow did in his training, with essential elements of jazz music-making in general.

The simplest building blocks of music are chords, tones that involve several notes. Chords can be developed in certain sequences deemed appropriate according to conventions of any given musical idiom. Such sequences can be shaped in certain ways, again to idiom-specific conventions, to form basic tunes, melodies, or songs. The improviser proceeds on a certain chord and plays sequences of notes known among jazz players as "riffs" or "runs." To the casual listener these runs may sound extemporaneous, but in fact, as already noted, jazz musicians spend much time by themselves perfecting a personal repertoire of runs which they may combine or vary within the limits of jazz conventions when they perform.[7]

---

7. Sudnow began to build his personal repertoire at a very early stage in his training (see 1978, pp. 28–29, 47).

But it is in the playing of a riff or run that the contextual reflexivity of the jazz performance becomes clear. The key insight is that any given chord provides a musical starting point from which certain possibilities can be pursued. Regarding improvisation in terms of musical skills on the piano keyboard, Sudnow (1981, pp. 23–29) describes these possibilities as pathways for his fingers to travel, that is, pathways for musical development that are consistent with the jazz conventions. Throughout *Ways of the Hand*, Sudnow shows readers how experienced jazz pianists do not have to think through these pathways. Instead, as they learn their skills they come to feel them "on their fingertips." Since each pathway also allows for a range of variations and alterations, there are innumerable though again not unlimited possibilities open to a musician for runs or riffs on any given chord. However, here is where the contextual reflexivity comes in. A run consists of a series of notes played in succession. Therefore, when only a few notes have been played, a performer has created a context that narrows down appropriate subsequent notes (i.e., notes that sound right to the trained jazz ear). Thus, from one note to the next, a run has a contextually reflexive quality, each note relying on its predecessors in order to sound right, and then providing the context for the next note to fit in. Of course, the number of possible next notes is not predetermined by the context as is true in a properly played game of solitaire. Nonetheless, to borrow solitaire's terminology, each note in a run draws upon a musical tableau, and in turn, alters that tableau as well. Of course, one run does not comprise an entire improvisation. At the end of a run the player makes a transition to a new opening note of another run and opens up a new round of possibilities and thus the contextual reflexivity of a new run begins. And there is a contextual connection between runs as well since each is derived from notes in the same or a related chord.

Like solitaire, then, jazz improvisation proceeds in contextually reflexive moves. But this is not the only similarity between the two as forms of solitary action. Recall that the moves in a game of solitaire are structured by a set of standard rules that the player has learned before the game begins. Though the structuration of jazz improvisation has none of the deterministic qualities of tightly defined rules, it should be apparent that jazz improvisation is no anarchic enterprise.[8] The basis of this structuration, of course, is formed by the conventions of jazz themes. Such conventions are rarely found in codified form. Musicians generally learn them on their own, no doubt listening to jazz recordings and performances, similar to the development of the ability to hear and transcribe tunes into notes that Faulkner and Becker describe. The important thing is that all jazz musicians master these conventions. Thus, a jazz improvisation, even an improvisation by someone as boldly original as Thelonious Monk, who advanced beyond received jazz conventions in many ways, still sounds like jazz, whereas a classical work such as, say, J. S. Bach's *Art of the Fugue*, for all of its variations on a theme, can never be mistaken for any kind of jazz at all.[9]

Solitary though they are, playing solitaire and mastering the craft involved in jazz improvisation exhibit two traits that mark them as forms of disciplined human conduct at large: contextual

8. This is one reason why Faulkner and Becker (2009, p. 26) describe improvisation as a synthesis of originality and conformity.

9. Even to the untutored ear, very few classical musicians cross the border between classical and jazz techniques. The most famous are George Gershwin in America and Darius Milhaud in France. Importing classical elements into jazz is a bit more common. Dave Brubeck (who studied with Milhaud) is well known for his classically tinged jazz compositions. Less well known but still remarkable are Jacques Loussier and Claude Bolling, who translated classical melodies and counterpoint techniques into the jazz idiom. My thanks to Eviatar Zerubavel for an introduction to Bolling and Loussier's music that is as charming as it is adventurous to the jazz newcomer's ear.

reflexivity and structuration. But a third item may be added to this list: an intense sense of involvement with the activity as it unfolds. Recall here the social psychological quality of solitaire that can calm jittery nerves, suspend troubling thoughts, and delay completion of onerous tasks. Sudnow's text is suffused with a similar sense of involvement. His central notion that jazz improvisers produce free-flowing streams of reflexively unfolding musical runs and phrases suggest something akin to Goffman's (1967, p. 113) "socialized trance" in conversation. Sudnow's central idea that jazz flows from the fingers rather than a purely mental direction suggests a concentrated coordination of body and mind that leaves little spare attention for anything else. True, the practicing musician's fingers may hit the wrong keys, or he may grow confused, in either case creating a break in the involvement. But even here a good deal of attention is required to pick up the musical threads. But when the music-making proceeds smoothly, the jazz player grows absorbed in a special way. At a pivotal moment in the development of his musical skills, Sudnow (1981, p. 93) describes how after a long period of development in which he awkwardly worked out his fingering routes, he reached a level of competency where mind and body came together:

> Now I may play rapidly along, singing the jazz with my fingertips, fully involved in a singing. . . . caught up in the music. At the same time, indeed in precise synchrony, I may without looking at the keyboard visualize the notes being played, the names of the notes, seeing the spellings of the melodies being played.

The telling phrase is "caught up in the music." Indeed, there is in this passage a hint of the kind of optimal experience that

Mihaly Csikszentmihalyi (1990) terms "flow."[10] (A more extensive discussion of "flow" appears in chapter 5.) This is not to naively suggest that jazz improvisation routinely generates optimal experiences of any kind. No doubt, even great musicians get distracted by their own errors or stop to play a phrase in a different way. Nonetheless, that optimal experiences are even possible suggests the power of the action as it unfolds to draw players in and engage them in the performance.

One final point on these examples. Though both exhibit reflexivity, structuration, and the capacity to involve the actor, which I will momentarily suggest are three main elements of solitary action, I have used these examples not because they are necessarily typical of all solitary actions, but rather because they illustrate in bold relief some of the elements of action with which I shall be concerned below. Indeed, as discussion develops, especially in chapters 4 and 5, it should become clear that structuration and the capacity to engage the actor are variable traits of different forms of solitary action. This is implicitly evident even here inasmuch as the move-by-move development of a properly played game of solitaire is far more tightly structured than the loosely structured jazz improvisation that offers the musician several different directions to go, in accordance with jazz conventions, at almost every turn.[11] Moreover, though solitaire and jazz improvisation are both absorbing solitary activities, many others do not hold the individual's attention equally well. For example, the true musical neophyte just learning her scales is

10. Sudnow might well resist this description. Like most ethnomethodologists, Sudnow (1978, p. 153) declares a moratorium on psychological insights of any kind. But the psychic quality of the experience he describes is hard to deny.

11. Even contextual reflexivity itself, though ordinarily the sine qua non of all forms of action, is not always present in solitary action. It will emerge in chapter 4 that some highly repetitive and routine forms of action (e.g., assembly line production work) create little or no context at all.

almost certain to be less absorbed by what she is doing than she will be when she has mastered her basic skills that then free her to get involved in music-making per se.

THE ELEMENTS OF SOLITARY ACTION

Step-by-step reflexive production of context, structuration, and the power of behavior to engage and absorb an actor's attention comprise three of the four elements of solitary action I now wish to discuss in a more generally conceptual way. To these elements I shall add one more: namely, the presence or absence of ongoing social processes, for example, externally directed work assignments and interpersonal aspects of ongoing activities. Together these four items comprise the elements in a conceptual framework. But before turning to the model and its elements, let me say a few words about my basic assumption.

I believe that how we behave when disengaged from others and how we behave in conjunction with others share fundamental common traits. Of course, common sense tells us that these two orders of behavior are not the same. People coordinate with each other when producing conversation, mass behavior, and interpersonal activities of all kinds. In interaction, for example, actors take turns producing locally reflexive contexts. No single individual, no matter how dominant or skillful she may be, controls every turn at talk, and thus no actor completely directs the course of context development as it unfolds in a conversational encounter. As I define solitary behavior, individuals who are disengaged from others enact and thereby control a sequence of moves of indefinite length, extending, expanding, redirecting, and shifting the development of a context with no move-by-move input from anyone else. Put another way, my assumption is that when we look past who coordinates and controls context formation, human beings do not behave so differently in their solitary activities as in their dealings with others. It is not as if we go through a metamorphosis of some kind, as if we were swarming caterpillars or schooling tadpoles under one set of conditions, and solitary butterflies or hopping frogs after a transformation. The conditions are certainly different in coordinated and solitary behavior, but we retain and apply common ways and means of action nonetheless.

Why underscore this assumption here? Mainly because the invisibility of solitary action among the leading lights in the study of basic traits of interaction (see chapter 2) predisposes sociologists to regard engagement with others as a necessary condition for behavior of all kinds. Garfinkel, Goffman, and Mead fix our attention on how we collaborate and accommodate our behavior. If those who closely attend and analyze behavior fail to note that playing solitaire or jazz solos or performing any of the myriad of other solitary activities mentioned elsewhere in this book are just as much forms of behavior as playing poker or performing in a musical ensemble, then it is quite likely that a much larger body of those who study social life miss the same point.

In the rest of this chapter I will expand upon each of the four analytical elements of solitary action in turn. The reader should bear in mind that this broad overview of the elements of solitary action leaves a great deal of room for variation in individual practices, activities, and sequences of action. Except for the distinction between continuing social processes on the one hand and solitary activity that concludes with the individual's solitary behavior on the other, I do not propose to discuss these variations at any great length. Variation becomes crucial in chapters 4 and 5, where discussion turns to differences in categorical forms of solitary activities. For example: while I shall discuss the capacity of an activity to hold the individual's attention without reference to variation in the present chapter, in chapter 4 I shall discuss one category of solitary activities (a category that includes the game of solitaire) that captures and holds the actor's attention in compelling ways and another category of solitary activities that I term regimens, in which the capacity to hold the individual's attention is very weak or entirely absent.

Reflexive Production of Context

The reflexive unfolding of move after move is what provides a broad variety of solitary actions with an orderly pattern. This move-by-move reflexive unfolding of orderly patterns is found in coordinated activities such as: in conversation, in the bid and raise pattern of auction, in the play-by-play development of a game of basketball, or in the joke-laugh-joke sequencing of a development of a dialogue between a stand-up comedian and an audience. We find the same pattern in solitary activities such as the move-by-move progression of a hand of solitaire and the succession of notes in a run in jazz improvisation, as described above. It is also evident in the place-by-place search by an individual for lost auto keys; in the step-by-step preparation of a stew, soup, or salad by a person alone in the kitchen; in the item-by-item completion of a crossword puzzle; or even in the paragraph-by-paragraph, story-by-story, section-by-section browse through a newspaper or a website. In every case actors move reflexively, creating context, moving ahead in relation to that context, and altering or shifting the context with each move. Though it is generally true (as Garfinkel, 1967, Ch. 8, suggests) that humans rarely develop rigidly logical and tightly integrated contexts, solitaire comes close and so does the step-by-step, draft-by-draft composition of a scientific research report or a bureaucratic memo. My point is that however loosely or tightly organized the step-by-step production of context in solitary actions may be, context formation maintains an order within action whenever it occurs.

Structuration: Cultural Patterns and Morality in Solitary Action

The structuration of action may be understood as the missing link in most analyses of everyday contextual reflexivity. If we observe action unfolding exclusively on a step-by-step basis, it is easy to miss the fact that individuals are producing culturally shaped patterns, that is, patterns that share traits (e.g., elements of form, teleology, symbolic significance, or connotation) with patterns produced by a smaller or larger group of other people now or in the past who collectively comprise a culture or subculture of some kind. These cultural patterns are not always easy to explicitly define. As novices, jazz improvisers learn which runs and transitions "sound like jazz" by tacitly absorbing the musical skills and shaping them in unique ways, thereby "making it their own." The same holds for other solitary creative artists: novice writers, painters, sculptors, and the like, who study and absorb the pattern-making skills of others. No two artists, working by themselves, may ever produce exactly the same work, and some of their works are widely regarded as better than others. Nevertheless, just as all jazz players play runs that sound like jazz, all picaresque novels or all coming-of-age stories share certain elements in common, as do all cubist paintings or all statues that honor public heroes. Any artistic genre requires certain skills that infuse common traits and patterns in the work.

The solitary activity of everyday actors is much the same: shared skills weave common forms and meanings into all behavior save for the truly disorganized doings of the cognitively impaired, the demented, and the deranged. Take a few prosaic examples. Each morning millions of Americans go through the rituals of bathing by themselves. There are of course idiosyncrasies in how they go about these humble acts. Still, most people clean and groom their bodies in similar ways: using a shower fixture, water, soap, shampoo, conditioner, toothbrush, razor, comb, hairbrush, and an electric dryer, not to mention cosmetics, lotions, and other beauty and grooming aids. Medieval European peasants would lack the skills to use at least some of these implements. The structuration of their hygienic routines would rely on different skills. Likewise, each week or month in most households, someone performs the necessary chore of paying bills and keeping accounts. The patterns here are more rigid. Like playing solitaire, there is often only one right way to keep the household books. Notice that none of these skillful behaviors is produced ad hoc in the reflexive moves of context formation. Widely shared skills come into play and for this reason millions of people standing alone in front of their bathroom mirrors or sitting alone with their bills and checkbooks (more recently assorted devices such as computers, smart phones, etc.) produce activities that share traits and patterns in common.

Processes of structuration rely on socially acquired skills. (We should also note the presence of some universally available pragmatic skills such as those employed by Robinson Crusoe.) But in discussing these skills, a significant distinction between solitary action and interpersonal behavior must be made. The question that prompts the distinction is this: what shapes the performance of social skills so that various instances of behavior share traits and patterns with others? Interaction, it must be said, has a broader array of resources to ensure that skills are deployed and practices enacted according to common cultural conventions. How so? Simply because when two or more actors are mutually engaged they can monitor their respective behaviors and observe aberrant practices, such as improper or inappropriate language, music played incorrectly or incompetently, and so on. Erving Goffman (1967, pp. 113–136) and Talcott Parson (1951, pp. 10–12), a sociological odd couple if ever there was one, both stressed the importance for correct behavior of the mutual reconnaissance and sanctioning within dyads and small groups.[12] Obviously, no contextual monitoring and sanctioning goes on when actors are on their own. If a bather fails to use soap to bathe, it is quite possible that no one will notice. If a jazz musician practicing alone plays a run of notes that doesn't work as jazz, no one will object. In some cases of course, others will eventually get to monitor the outcome or solitary behavior. Household bookkeepers may make mistakes while alone but eventually the bank balance will catch up with them and their creditors will hold them sternly to account. Nevertheless, no one is on the scene when they make the mistakes in the first place.

But setting aside questions of delayed monitoring, which I will address later on in terms of the flow of large social processes through solitary activities, the question remains: What ensures that actors will apply the proper skills to the structuration of solitary action? In response, let me propose two aspects of structuration, each of which is in a broad sense moral though in distinct and different respects. The first is a matter of the constraints of technique, the second, and more familiar, is a matter of the constraints of solitary conscience.

As Giddens observes (1984, pp. 304–310; Cohen, 1989, pp. 221–228), the same skills that enable us to produce routine

---

12. Goffman's notion of "involvement obligations" and Parsons's "double contingency of interaction" are, if not conceptually homologous, then at least quite compatible, though Goffman, unlike Parsons, spends a great deal more time analyzing how actors fail to fulfill their obligations and what happens as a result.

practices constrain us as well. But how so? Simply put, when individuals acquire a culturally common skill they learn that there are right ways and wrong ways to mobilize those skills. This is the morality of technique in the sense that the competent person must conform within certain latitudes to an often-tacit code of conduct to put these skills to work. The latitude that the morality of technique allows may vary a great deal. Managing household budgets or playing solitaire impose rigid constraints, reading a newspaper or preparing food is less restrictive, and improvising jazz not only leaves room for variation but requires that unique elements be created through the use of culturally shared skills. But there are limits to improvisation as well. In the absence of the common traits woven into jazz there would be no orderly structuration at all. Not only would this violate the morality of technique, it would create an acute moment of behavioral disorganization that risks the psychic consequences of anomie. The fact that most people do not experience this disorganization and anomie when they are by themselves is evidence in itself for the effects of the morality of technique. This is not to say that we are always aware of this discipline. To the contrary, some skillful practices when we are by ourselves are enacted via habits and unreflective routines. But others, such as finding a bug in a computer program or a fix for a balky washing machine can require as much correct conduct as any morally compelling code of interpersonal conventions.

The morality of technique may operate tacitly. But in a surprising though by no means unlimited number of practices, doing things the right way takes on a moral quality that affects our activity as a matter of conscience rather than technique. Consider a student practicing the piano alone. Let us say he makes a mistake. There is nothing to stop him from simply playing on. Yet many students conscientiously stop playing and repeat the passage much as if a stern conductor were overseeing their work. Or consider a person who lives alone yet cleans the house carefully without taking shortcuts. For these subjects to act improperly would provoke a twinge of guilt. Now I don't mean to suggest that everyone is imbued with a strong conscience when alone, nor that every form of structuration makes morally compelling claims. To the contrary, without the morality of technique, I suspect that conscience by itself would not constrain individuals in anything more than a haphazard fashion. Many people who live alone do not always keep a clean and tidy house, though they may do so on occasion. Much the same is probably true of most other morally tinged solitary activities as well. Nonetheless, the power of morality when it does intrude should not be underestimated. Consider what may be one of the most moralized of all modern self-imposed practices, maintaining a diet. I do not refer here to why people diet; no doubt certain interpersonal motives or reasons may be involved. I refer, rather, to the practices involved in dieting per se, practices that the majority of dieters perform by themselves. I think it safe to say that almost all dieters cheat on their diets and feel pangs of guilt for their pleasure. But what is the more relevant aspect of dieting here is the struggle in which dieters engage to suppress their appetite for fattening foods and thereby to avoid the guilt they would impose on themselves were they to give in to temptation.

Dieting, like many other solitary activities fraught with virtue and vice, derives from secular moral codes embedded in mundane ways of life. But moral derivation of solitary practices is nothing new. Most religions have regarded solitude as a venue well suited to meditation, prayer, and communion with their deity. Religiously inspired fasting (e.g., during the Muslim holy month of Ramadan and the Jewish high holy day of Yom Kippur) is also a morally fraught activity that requires a certain set of solitary practices of self-restraint. Most religions instruct the faithful in a variety of contexts, creating morally infused practices and routines through which they can worship, pray, or find spiritual communion with God. While it would be correct to simply gloss these practices as highly moralized in the Durkheimian sense that the faithful perform them with some sense of moral obligation, the actual practice often creates the context in which the devout experience the morally compelling aura of the divine or at least the moral power that emanates from the divine. For example, consider the practice common in certain Jewish groups of saying silent prayers in Hebrew when the worshiper has no facility in the Hebrew language. What is happening here as the properly trained worshiper recites and often chants or sings sotto voce (with as much accuracy as possible) what to her are meaningless tropes? In effect, as the words and melodies are whispered in the obligatory form, she is generating within herself the experience of divine presence. But to produce this experience she must pray in the liturgically correct way, using skills that she has mastered only as ritual rather than in an everyday form. Yet these ritual skills are not only morally obligatory, they are morally compelling as well. There is, in effect, a morally and spiritually infused example of the skillful production of an unfolding solitary context.[13]

Ongoing Processes and Self-Contained Activities

Structuration brings society's influence into solitary activity via the skills we use that enable us to situate and produce our

13. I refrain from mentioning Buddhist practices of solitary meditation here. While Buddhist meditation is among the most disciplined and constrained forms of solitary activity, the status of Buddhist spirituality as a religion has bedeviled sociologists of religion since Weber and Durkheim's classic works. It would unnecessarily complicate present discussion to get involved in that controversy here. Those interested in Buddhist practices in solitude may wish to consult Michal Pagis (2010).

actions on a reflexive, move-by-move basis. Skills are necessary conditions for whatever we do by ourselves. But skills are insufficient in themselves to determine the sociological character of what we do. We also mistake accounts of the social provenance of solitary conduct. By provenance I mean the place of origin, the terminus a quo, of solitary action. A binary distinction will help pin down what is at stake here. On the one hand, by virtue of the freedom that the lack of surveillance in disengagement from others allows, the provenance of some solitary activities may be self-contained. But on the other hand, even when actors are disengaged from and unmonitored by others, their activities may originate in ongoing interpersonal processes and relationships. Though we have already considered certain moral constraints that are implicated in the skills through which solitary actions are performed, when the provenance of solitary action arises in the external, interpersonal realm, a second set of moral commitments may encourage or even fix solitary action on certain courses and discourage or even forestall solitary action from going astray.

Playing solitaire is a simple example of a self-contained activity. Presume that in this case an actor plays solitaire to avoid being bored. Now we could look to the external environment and tie the actor's boredom to interpersonal circumstances. But this seems to be stretching a point for two reasons: first, boring situations sometimes arise due to unintended consequences, such as waiting for others who are detained due to bad weather or other unscheduled events. Second, even when others have intentionally created a boring situation, say, in solitary imprisonment, playing solitaire is only one option among others that may keep actors occupied. Moreover, solitaire not only begins at the discretion of the actor, it ends with the actor as well, leaving no direct consequences.

Any given culture is likely to have a variety of self-contained simple activities to provide some relief from boredom, anxiety, and restlessness at large. In our own culture, airport shops stock most of their shelves with all sorts of what I shall discuss in chapter 4 as "engrossments," from puzzles and games to undemanding formulaic novels. Solitary physical exercise is also a self-contained activity as are many amateur arts and crafts, household do-it-yourself projects, and a long list of similar projects for self-improvement or material improvement.

Internally bounded characteristics distinguish self-contained activities from ongoing social processes or relationships. Though a person may work on various aspects of such multi-phase processes on her own when she is disengaged from others, it remains only one phase of an ongoing sequence that involves other actions and interactions. The terminus a quo of the action is located before its solitary phase. Moreover, many (though not necessarily all) solitary phases of multi-phase processes continue beyond the solitary activity as well. Various kinds of white-collar work offer straightforward examples. Consider accounting work. It is the nature of their work for accountants to spend a good deal of time managing and auditing financial records by themselves. However, these financial records always relate back to their client's prior transactions and plans. The accountant may work alone, but her work is simply one phase in her client's ongoing economic life. If we want to further complicate matters, we can also consider the accountant's place in a division of labor in an accounting firm. In work on a large set of books, for example, several accountants may perform different functions while working alone and later combine their results when their solitary tasks are done. In any event, many kinds of solitary white-collar tasks are actually phases in ongoing social processes.

Numerous other kinds of work share this multi-phase quality. Students, for example, come together for classes where they may interact with their teachers and classmates as part of the learning process. But at some point most students break away to read and write assignments on their own, and if all goes well, the interpersonal and solitary phases of learning form a single coherent educational process. Meanwhile, a related multi-phase process takes place on the other side of the lectern or desk. Classes, office appointments, and staff meetings constitute interpersonal phases of teaching. Lesson planning, lecture writing, assignment preparing, and exam grading typically are carried out by teachers or faculty members on their own. Homemakers who have children in school cycle through phases of busy interaction, with children departing in the morning and returning after school and the homemaker taking care of solitary tasks in between.

Readers of chapter 2 may recall my objections to George Herbert Mead's premise that the life of the mind is little more than an arena for ongoing interpersonal processes. In my view, Mead fails to notice the significance of self-contained activities. Nonetheless, Mead deserves much credit for the notion that many significant processes cycle in and out of what he termed external and internal phases during the course of everyday life. Perhaps the most ubiquitous of all social processes in modern Western societies are transacted as phases in personal relationships, such as those between children and caregivers, extremely close friends, or intimate couples. Iconic images of close relationships present people engaging in gestures or rituals of togetherness and strong ties, for example, confiding, sharing, celebrating, or mourning together. Like other iconic images, these are true enough for symbolic purposes but they obscure as much as they reveal, namely, how people work on aspects of their relationships by themselves. Consider, for example, an intimate couple in the early days of discovery when a relationship begins. Even in the intense intimacy of new love, partners spend time apart thinking fond thoughts, spinning happy plans, and anticipating their next encounter with their beloved. Does this solitary excitement always improve the relationship? Not necessarily. Infatuated fantasies can raise expectations that no relationship can meet for very long. The only certainty about what goes on in the solitary phases of a relationship is that the results will find their way into the couple's interaction when they meet again.[14] To say that part of what goes on in a relationship happens while the participants are disengaged is a generalized way of referring to processes that are very specific and real. Let me then supply a brief example. This one is from the novel *Room Temperature* by the uniquely gifted American novelist Nicholson Baker. In the following passage Baker (1984, p. 25) presents a newlywed husband who describes a means he employs to discover some of his new wife's tastes in domestic goods.

> Covertly I would study her as she looked at a shelf full of gravy boats at an antique store, watching her eye movements and trying to learn, without having her spell it out, which gravy boats she liked and which she rejected and which attracted her and in what order; and I did the same as we flipped through a glossy house magazine together.

Though the husband obviously cares a great deal for his wife, he studies her silently by himself. Moreover, a disengaged condition is of the essence of this act. Were he to ask her directly to tell him

14. Whether pre-modern intimate relationships, which often were less encompassing than intimate bonds today, included significant solitary phases is an interesting question that could be investigated through the study of diaries and correspondence.

or show him what she likes or dislikes, he would not have the implicit but telling evidence that he gleans from watching her unselfconsciously reveal her tastes. And, no doubt, in due course the husband will make use of what he learns in this way. Perhaps he will use his covertly acquired knowledge to surprise his wife with a well-chosen gift, or perhaps he will surprise her in conversation by displaying his silently collected insights into her likes and dislikes. Of course, Baker supplies his narrator with a degree of sensitive observational skill that few of us can match. Do most newlywed husbands possess the inclination and ability to gauge the tastes of their wives in such a clever, covert way? No, probably not. Let Baker's example then epitomize rather than typify those things regarding relationships that couples do on their own. It suffices to say that in more mundane and varied ways, what goes on when actors are by themselves is part of what either builds or breaks a modern relationship.

When what actors do by themselves involves personal or occupational commitments, additional layers of moral obligation are implicated in solitary activities. Compare playing solitaire with completing a work assignment on deadline. A person who plays solitaire may play properly or cheat, but assuming she is not procrastinating, she does not need to take into account any obligation to anyone else. However, when a worker works on deadline, this means that she has committed herself to organize her time and effort so as to put the finished products in the hands of others by the expected date. Even if the worker meets deadlines in order to keep her job, in effect she has made a promise or given her word. To put the point in Durkheimian terms, moral commitments are implicated in work contracts of all kinds including agreements to complete assignments on deadline without supervision. True, there are shirkers and cynics in solitary conditions just as anywhere else who take an instrumental approach and fail to deliver on deadline if no one monitors when their work is received. But what is more remarkable is how often people discipline themselves to finish jobs after hours of working at home at night simply because of commitments they have made to finish a job by themselves. Though solitary work involves underlying moral commitments, certain forms of solitary behavior are part of what holds social relationships together as well. As noted above, primary caregivers spend time by themselves cooking, cleaning, and doing other chores out of nothing more than the moral obligation to maintain a decent household for their children. Domestic partners divide up other chores into solitary assignments as well. There are many more individuals than couples in the queues in supermarkets and the waiting rooms of auto repair shops. Likewise, it only takes one person to vacuum the floor, make the beds, mow the lawn, and do many other domestic chores. When all goes well, we carry out many of our solitary chores as habits. However, some solitary activities are too stressful and difficult to rely on habits at all. Though close relationships develop enduring qualities over time, the moral events that matter within relationships are multi-phase processes, parts of which are interpersonal, and parts of which go on when parties to the relationship go off by themselves. For example, a quarrel usually goes through an interpersonal phase where parties establish their grievances, explicitly or implicitly charging the other with failing to abide by their reciprocal moral obligations and to their relationships at large. If and when the parties reconcile, this too will happen in face-to-face interaction. However, if the situation is at all serious, between the time of the quarrel and the reconciliation, the parties will spend time mulling over the details. In some cases these reflections serve to confirm grievances and harden feelings. But in other cases time spent apart provides enough distance from the give and take of interaction for people to reframe their actions from the other party's point of view and reevaluate their own moral position. Without this solitary period, it is safe to say it would be much more difficult for people to reestablish a mutual harmony and put quarrels to rest.

Though Arlie Russell Hochschild focuses on "emotion work" and discusses the moral dimension of solitary activity only as an aspect of her own concerns, in *The Managed Heart* (1983, Chs. 2–3; see also 1979) she nonetheless offers an especially instructive example of the moral significance of what actors do by themselves. "Feeling rules" provide the moral linchpin of her theory. Feeling rules are expectations people share of what kinds of emotions should be conveyed in various social situations. Moral dilemmas arise when an individual feels a deviant emotion, that is, a feeling other than the feeling she is expected to convey. Emotion work involves some effort on the individual's part to organize her behavior so that she will express the expected feeling and meet the shared emotional norm. "Deep acting," the most effective type of emotion work, is performed when the individual manipulates her feelings so that she is able to express the morally appropriate feeling in a sincerely felt way. Emotion work is thus an act of morally inspired personal transformation. And the salient point here is that while it is certainly possible for people to manipulate their feelings in confidential conversations, most of Hochschild's empirical examples recount her informants' reports of instances where they manipulated their feelings on their own, finding situations in their personal experiences that allowed them to emotionally relate to the feelings of others, or using their imaginations to the same end. Once she has reframed the situation via these recollected or imagined feelings, she is prepared to express the morally obligatory feeling in a sincere, unforced way. Here again, the internal activity is only one phase in a process that has external phases as well.

Two Mechanisms of Solitary Involvement

Involvement is the last element of solitary action in my analysis here. Involvement can be conceived in two ways. On the one hand, we can consider how the individual involves herself in an action, or more to the point, in how she involves herself in the reflexive production of activity. This first approach, which deals with psychological ways in which actors invest themselves in what they do, appeals to our intuition that involvement is an act of will, an effort at selective concentration through which an actor keeps her mind attentive to the point of being immersed in whatever is going on. Involvement, defined psychologically, is a sustained act of attention. Attention, in turn, is to cite the classic psychological definition by William James ([1890] 1981, p. 381–382):

> The taking possession by the mind, in clear and vivid form, of one out of what seem several simultaneously possible objects or trains of thought. Focalization, concentration of consciousness are of its essence. It implies withdrawal from some things in order to deal effectively with others and it has a real opposite in the confused, dazed, scatterbrained state [of mind].

So long as the individual sustains the attention, we are dealing with involvement in James's psychological sense.[15] The sociological definition, though not at all mutually exclusive from the psychological definition, is less intuitive but no less significant. At issue here is how an activity, anything from playing solitaire to improvising a riff on a jazz theme to reading a book, holds our attention. This seems counterintuitive because it suggests that forms of conduct can hold our attention as if they have powers of their own. In a certain sociological

---

15. This rules out the brief moments of startled attention, for example, a moment to identify the source of an unexpected flash of light or a loud noise.

sense, I propose that such holding powers are real. Moreover, I suggest that activities can involve individuals and hold their attention in several different ways, and I shall presently bring this argument to bear on my key question here, namely: How do solitary activities involve us in their moves and practices? But first a few words of clarification about the psychological side of involvement.

Were we not a species endowed with psychic capacities to focus our perceptions and thoughts and to hold them so that we can continue doing something, we would be unable to stay involved in anything at all. Indeed, there comes a point when various forms of dementia have taken a sufficient toll on the brain that its victims lose the ability to stay involved and their attention wanders erratically both when they try to speak with others and when they try to do things by themselves. Quite understandably, psychologists have devoted a great deal of effort to studying how actors pay attention. Given the results of dementia and other forms of brain damage, it is now generally accepted by neuropsychologists that when we include low-level types of attention as well as attention in more sophisticated forms (a useful distinction to which I shall return in chapter 4), neurobiologically, the alert human brain is attentive and involved in doing things all day long (see Edelman, 2006, p. 93; Damasio, 1999, p. 91, pp. 86–94 passim). Neuropsychologists still disagree theoretically over many aspects of attention. However, it would not be surprising to find that it is human nature in a physiological sense to invest at least enough attention in what we are doing and in what is going on to keep ourselves psychologically engaged and cognitively organized.

However, once neuropsychologists and cognitive psychologists have learned more than they presently know, and even if it turns out that involvement is indeed a fundamental need of our species, we will still need to know much more than psychology alone can tell us about what makes social activities more or less compelling. Is motivation a factor? Yes and no. Certainly motivation stirs people to begin concentrating on something. But strong motivation is an exceptional occurrence in everyday life, generally found only in unusually demanding situations. With the exception of what I shall term "regimens" in chapter 4,[16] people generally stay involved in something because the activity holds them rather than because they hold their concentration, come what may. In other words, we need to take a turn to the sociology of solitary action to discover what involves people and how their attention is held. This last proposition sounds like a hypostatized reading of Durkheim, in which social things, in this case social activities, grab our attention like magnets that hold iron filings to an orderly pattern. But the static imagery of the metaphor belies the dynamic character of the activities in which we become involved. Perhaps it would be better to say that activities carry us with them, in which case a better metaphor would be that when we are involved in an activity it is as if we are carried along by a song we are singing, or a book we are reading, or a game we are playing. So then the question becomes: By what mechanism do activities carry us along? And what makes carrying power especially important in the analysis of what individuals do when they are by themselves? Ultimately, I think that three mechanisms can carry us forward in activities. The three are not mutually exclusive. However, one is inoperative in solitary forms of conduct, which makes the other two especially important as far as the sociology of solitary action is concerned.

16. Regimens are defined in chapter 4 as categorical forms of solitary activity that lack the ability to hold the individual's attention. In chapter 4 I shall raise the question of how individuals cope with these forms of solitary activity. As I shall indicate, there are different ways of coping, depending on the traits of different kinds of regimens.

Interaction's special ability to involve and engross is the mechanism that is inoperative in solitary action. Involvement in this sense deeply impressed Erving Goffman, who explored it at great length when he studied focused interaction and distracted behavior during interaction (1963, Chs. 3–5; 1967, pp. 113–135) and referred to involvement elsewhere as a fundamental feature of the interaction order (1974, pp. 142, 345, 347 passim; 1983, pp. 2–3). Ironically, Goffman, who did his best to modulate the affects of human psychology in his analysis of conduct, defined involvement in terms reminiscent of the definition of attention advanced by William James. But the deeper, and for present purposes more germane, irony is that despite his psychological definition, Goffman understood better than any other sociologist has ever understood that interaction has the power to induce not merely involvement but what Goffman terms "a socialized trance." He goes on to maintain that interaction "has a life of its own and makes demands on its own behalf" (1967, p. 113). Goffman here intuitively sensed quite well that there is more than psychology at issue in how interaction makes demands on those who participate. When people engage in face-to-face interactions they bring cultural expectations that others will attend to their contributions and that they will reciprocate in turn and in kind. These are the demands that produce the intense, spontaneous involvement of the "socialized trance." There can be no question that people do bring normative expectations regarding involvement to interaction and that these expectations and the surveillance and sanctions through which they are enforced give interaction a unique power to compel involvement, a power that solitary behavior lacks.[17] So now we need to pose the pivotal

17. As do some (not all) collective forms of behavior where the group is too large for actors to directly monitor the attention of all members of their audience.

question: If solitary activities cannot rely on collective expectations of attention, how do they manage to engage individuals and carry them along? After all, to extend my previous point, if solitary behavior depended only upon sheer willpower, only in unusual situations would ordinary individuals rely on their own motivation to do things on their own. Lacking that, there would be nothing to keep solitary actors focused and engaged.

To see what does carry people along in their solitary doings let us return to the game of solitaire, which turns out to be highly instructive because it incorporates in an elementary form both of the basic mechanisms of involvement at work in solitary activities at large. It bears repetition here that people play solitaire primarily for its hypnotic powers. Given that solitaire possesses this quality, it would appear that interaction is not the only kind of behavior that can induce a socialized trance. How does this simple game generate these dramatic effects? To begin, bear in mind that solitaire is an auto-hypnotic activity. That is, actors must play the game to become involved. Playing is so essential to the hypnotic effect that it is safe to say that if individuals merely watched the game unfold according to pre-programmed software they would quickly grow bored, whereas when they deal, scan, match, and draw cards and thereby actually perform each move themselves they concentrate and pay close attention, sometimes for hours on end.

Two mechanisms are intrinsic to the play of the game area responsible for keeping players involved. The first is context formation, for which I have broken much ground earlier in the chapter. The second is the rhythm of the game, which deserves some special attention in itself.

Context formation first. Solitaire involves the actor in a tightly structured process of reflexivity. Each move the player makes, whether it be to scan the tableau, make a match, draw a new trio of cards, etc. must be situated in the previously established tableau. And, each move raises expectations that new matches may be available that were not possible before. The matches that are made provide the player with small increments of progress and open the possibility of more progress to come. Moreover, the initial deal to the seven stacks is well suited to begin the progress–possibility cycle because the statistical possibilities of the deal strongly favor some context-altering matches even before the first trio of cards is drawn. In this way the reflexive contextuality of the game draws the player on, keeps her involved, and carries her from one move to the next.

Now to rhythm. This mechanism too is intrinsic to the play of the game. But in this case it is not how moves are made, but the simple rhythm established as one move follows the next. This rhythm develops with experience; beginners may need to pause as they scan the tableau and match cards. But with experience, the player learns to scan and find matches quickly. When she reaches this point, once the initial tableau has been dealt, the game takes on its characteristic rhythm of scan-match, scan-match (repeated until all available matches are made), then draw-scan-match-scan-match, try again, and so on until the last match has been made. Though the reflexive production of context is a highly engrossing process in itself, the rhythmic pulse of play engrosses mind and body. The bodily rhythms are small: mainly movements of cards (manually or by a computerized pointing device); coordinated with these moves are sequential focusing and refocusing of the eyes as they anticipate and follow moves from spot to spot across the tableau. Other than these two rhythmic physical movements, all the individual has to do is fix her posture in position and stay put. The key to the hypnotic effect of the rhythm is its repetitive pattern. Even the most experienced player will lose this rhythm given any interruption. Momentarily retrieving an item that has fallen to the floor can break solitaire's seductive, rhythmic spell just as effectively as a frozen computer screen or a fire alarm.

Solitaire is misleading as an example of the hypnotic power of repetitive rhythms in one respect. The easiest and most effective way to induce hypnotic effects via solitary rhythmic activity is via repetitive cycles of athletic exercise. As a (very slow) jogger, I can testify to what is sometimes called the "runner's high," a feeling of solitary relaxation that in my case develops after 5–10 minutes of jogging at a very consistent pace. It must be said that this athletically induced trance differs quite a bit from the engrossment produced when playing solitaire. In my case, this state of isolation and relaxation allows me to either "go along for the ride" as it were, or simply to let my mind wander in peripatetic ways. Two qualities of repetitive athletic activities seem to be responsible for this relaxing effect. The rhythm itself, and endorphin, a secretion from the pituitary gland that is released during physical activity and serves as a kind of weak opiate. Though much more prosaic than endorphins, the second quality of rhythmic athletic activity may be just as necessary to their relaxing, hypnotic effects. I refer here to the simple fact that rhythmic activity often has the effect of isolating the individual from interruptions in the surrounding environment. This is true of jogging and cycling that move the body along too quickly for interruption by most stimuli. It is even more dramatically true for swimmers who enter another medium altogether. As one swimmer wrote on his blog:

> There is the swimmer's high that comes from the sensory deprivation associated with being in the water. Cut off from your surroundings, your mind slowly numbed from the repetition of lap after lap, your body cooled by the water, this sensation also can be very addicting (Leverenz, 2003).

Solitaire and rhythmic athletic activities are unusual in the hypnotic effects they produce. Though solitaire in particular illustrates the powers of involvement in solitary activities quite well, it obscures the considerable range of variation in the power of other solitary activities to engage the actor in a process and carry her along. In mentioning this variability I foreshadow the concerns of chapter 4, in which, among other matters of interest, I will deal at some length with activities such as school drills, factory work, and domestic work that often lack any ability to draw actors in and keep them involved. For now it is enough to say that both in terms of context formation and repetitive rhythms, some kinds of solitary activities are stronger than others.

CLOSING REMARKS: THE SOCIOLOGY OF SOLITARY ACTION

I began this chapter by asking: what are the basic traits that enable individuals to do things apart from the group? The chapter is organized to answer this question in full. But though the chapter is organized around the elements of solitary action, there is a second theme that is neither a counterpoint to the first nor just a leitmotif, but rather an inextricable pattern interwoven into everything I have had to say. The pattern has to do with the social shaping of solitary action, and it recurs in each of the analytical elements I have been discussing here. It may be worthwhile to highlight several of the social influences on solitary action that have come up along the way. In the first place, the question of how is it possible to act apart from the group is more sociological than it may seem. What could possibly be so sociological about asking questions about disengaged or detached activity? The answer lies in the way that action or behavior takes center stage rather than the Cartesian actor. Actions, not actors, are the units being analyzed throughout the chapter. I claim no originality for this strategy. Mead, Goffman, Garfinkel, and many others have been "decentering" the actor for quite a long time. All I have done is take the notion of action, where, for reasons set forth in chapter 2, none of these theorists chose to go.

The contextual reflexivity of action is not any more or less sociological than any other theory of action, but it is, from my point of view, the most elementary feature of behavior, the pivotal process in all social activity apart from the small subset that rely exclusively on rhythmic repetition. As for structuration, one of the latent keys to Giddens's conceptual schemes is that we build large-scale social patterns beyond our own recognition by means of our socially acquired skills. Structuration is embedded in the skills that allow us to produce reflexive contextual action. Garfinkel may have hidden society's influence on our skills behind brackets of ethnomethodological indifference, but his brackets, like all brackets, are impermanent barriers that can be removed just as freely as they can be imposed. Again, however, the significant thing here is that the discussion carries structuration into the solitary realm. Moreover, the very skills that we use in structuring our solitary actions bring one type of morality into solitary situations. The Durkheimian point then becomes clear: human beings are moral, at least in a minimal sense, simply because there are right ways and wrong ways to act, and ipso facto right kinds of social patterns and wrong kinds of latent social patterns that we can produce.

Chapter 4

Forms of Solitary Action: Peripatetics, Regimens, Engrossments

OVERVIEW

What do people do when they are by themselves but not engaged in thinking or reflecting on some matter in a focused and concentrated way? Though the question itself is not very difficult, it is not a question that comes readily to mind with regard to solitary action. Thinking, reflecting, solving problems, creating new things, these are the kinds of things we associate with what we do when we are detached from others. Surely that is what we do . . . on some occasions . . . at least for part of the time. But we can easily overestimate how much focused reflection we actually do. Consider here one of the world's iconic images of reflection, Auguste Rodin's *The Thinker*. The figure in this sculpture shows us what it takes to concentrate and reflect. His posture is tense and his major muscles are taut. His pose draws attention to his head, while his disengaged gaze suggests that his thoughts are focused on matters that either lie within or occupy a profound, abstract realm. Immobile though he is, he most definitely is exerting himself with sustained, strenuous effort. From all of this it is easy to see why in the symbolic culture of modern times *The Thinker* has come to represent a normative ideal of the best possible activity in which modern individuals can engage by themselves.

It doesn't take a moral philosopher to alert us to the fact that normative ideals and everyday life are two different things. It would be the height of hypocrisy for anyone who writes seriously, and therefore takes concentrated thought seriously, to deny the ideal that Rodin's *Thinker* represents. I have no intention to deny that ideal here. In terms of the sociology of solitary action, I am duty-bound to say that there is much that goes on that bears little or no resemblance to focused and concentrated solitary reflection and thought when modern actors are by themselves. Why not? To be fully engaged in solving or defining or pondering problems or intellectual dilemmas is hard work, especially when done by oneself. Even the most diligent writer knows that there is only a finite amount of time each day, generally well short of the eight-hour shift that other jobs entail, after which the quality of the writing tails off and it will be more productive to take a break or work less intensively at another task. For another thing, various conditions, social and otherwise, preclude many people from devoting solitary time to serious reflection. For some people it's the non-cognitive demands of their jobs, including manual labor and repetitive tasks in clerical work. For others it's their age: children may be too young to emulate *The Thinker*, senior citizens may possess a shorter attention span than they had at their disposal in their younger years. And this list of circumstances that impedes or diverts people from Rodin's ideal is hardly complete. Focused thought and concentrated reflection needs to be taken quite seriously in any sociology of action. For this reason, I have reserved the entirety of the next chapter to consider reflective activity at great length. In this chapter, however, I want to consider what we do by ourselves when our faculties of reason and reflection are set in an idle gear.

One of the surprising things about solitary activities is how many there are that do not require sustained, focused thought, and how diverse they are as well: solitary wandering in various contexts and locales, such as city streets, forests, supermarkets; surfing the web or reading magazines; along a very different line, we find many dull, unengaging solitary tasks at work, school, and in the home; again, along a different line, a broad variety of simple, solitary recreations, including the game of solitaire, as discussed in chapter 3, form another group.

Initially these activities may seem prosaic. After all, who doesn't know that assembly line work is boring, or that people often wander without any fixed destination when they take a walk in the woods? However, looking more closely at these forms raises some interesting questions within the sociology of solitary action, and in some cases in the general sociology of action at large. In the first place, as the organization of the preceding examples implies, the forms of solitary behavior at issue here fall into three general categories. Indeed, my first order of business in this chapter will be to devise a framework to classify both focused, reflective solitary activity as well as three distinctly different forms of behavior that diverge from Rodin's ideal. With this framework in hand, the more substantial issues in the chapter extend well beyond the classification per se. As will become evident along the way, each of the three forms of solitary action to be discussed introduce novel turns in the line of thought that adds something to our understanding of solitary action. In the case of wandering activities (which I shall call peripatetics) a question arises as to whether daydreams, fantasies, and other elliptical, loose-jointed mental activities count as social action. To this novel question, my answer is yes on some counts, but no on others. Consideration of boring tasks raises the question of how people cope and persist with the tedium of dull activities. The interesting issue here is that coping with boring, solitary tasks happens in three different ways, depending upon the more or less demanding nature of the tasks. Finally, with regard to simple but absorbing forms of solitary recreation (which I call engrossments) a question arises that expands upon the earlier analysis of solitaire. At issue now is: How do disparate activities such as crossword puzzles and formulaic fiction manage to capture the solitary individual's attention and keep her involved continuously for extended periods of time?

Beginning with Goffman and Garfinkel, the implicit motto of the sociology of action has been: there is more in simple forms of social behavior than meets the understanding eye. This chapter is undertaken in the spirit of that motto. To borrow one of Garfinkel's simplest, most incisive phrases, a good deal of social action is conducted in seen but unnoticed ways. I believe this to be true of the modest forms of solitary action that I shall discuss. Thus, my goal here is to notice what we see in prosaic solitary events.

FOUR FORMS OF SOLITARY ACTIVITIES

Two of the elements of solitary action identified in chapter 3 provide dichotomous dimensions for a two-by-two classification of basic forms of solitary activities. Though *forms* of solitary activities may sound synonymous with the *elements* of solitary action addressed in chapter 3, such is not the case. The elements discussed in chapter 3 (contextual reflexivity, structuration, strictly solitary or multiphase processes, and ability of practices to involve the actor) refer to analytically abstracted constituents of action in a manner analogous to the way physicists discuss the various constituents of the atom. The forms of solitary action

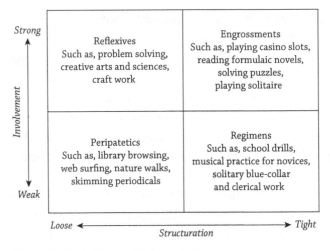

Figure 4.1: Basic Forms of Solitary Action.

referenced in Figure 4.1 are not analytically abstracted. Instead, the illustration presents four distinctly different categories (forms), each of which may include an indefinite number of specific solitary activities. Since the forms are general categories, the specific instances can be expected to vary. For example, the category of engrossments to be discussed later on in this chapter includes, among other examples, reading novels and solving jigsaw puzzles. The manifest differences between them notwithstanding, both share the two traits that classify them as engrossments as the category identified in Figure 4.1: that is, they engross the individual in an activity that proceeds in a tightly structured way. The two dichotomies used for classificatory purposes here originally appeared in chapter 3 as analytical elements of solitary action. Of course, as in all categorical dichotomies, some ambiguous cases should be expected here. However, for present purposes it is more important to establish the categories than to consider exceptions, and therefore I shall bracket the ambiguous cases here.

On the horizontal axis (see Figure 4.1), the tight/loose dichotomy refers to the structuration of a given form of behavior, that is, the extent to which the performance of the action allows less or more opportunity for the actor to vary practices or routines. Thus, tightly structured activities allow little room for variation, while loosely structured activities not only allow more room for variation but in many instances they may require the individual to improvise to a certain extent if the behavior is to be enacted at all. Here are two simple examples. On the one hand, driving a car is a tightly structured activity. Improvisations in driving practices can be dangerous. On the other hand, surfing the web is a loosely structured activity. There is no correct choice to move from one link to the next. Individuals must make their own moves.[1]

The strong/weak dichotomy on the vertical axis (see Figure 4.1) refers to the extent to which a given type of solitary activity engages individuals and keeps them involved as the action proceeds. As mentioned in chapter 3, this point of view on the capacity of practices to keep actors engaged brackets personal preferences and psychological matters such as motivation, personality differences, variations in innate abilities, and so on. Thus, a strong activity keeps individuals fully attentive and absorbed in the moves and sequences through which it unfolds, while a weak activity lacks this holding power so that little effort is required to break away at any time. The weakest activities of all, those I term regimens below, lack any holding power at all and individuals find them boring and dull as a result. Here are two contrasting examples: on the one hand, solving a crossword puzzle has a strong hold on the individual, as indicated by the number of people who stick with a puzzle for as long as it takes

---

1. The concept of structuration is, of course, considerably more complex than this dichotomy (see Cohen, 1989, pp. 219–221, passim).

to complete; on the other hand, solitary, highly routinized factory work holds no interest for the individual at all. For this type of factory work, there is no teleology or unfolding development of any kind with which to engage. Not all activities are weak to this extent, however. For example, a patron casually browsing library shelves for recreational reading may find nothing of interest along some aisles but discover a cluster of intriguing books elsewhere.

Cross-referencing structuration (loose/tight) along the horizontal axis and holding capacity (weak/strong) along the vertical axis, we arrive at the four categories indicated in Figure 4.1. I will consider three of the four categories below, reserving reflexives for the next chapter. However, a word about the terminology may be useful here. For three of the four categories, peripatetics, engrossments, and reflexives, in order to provide categorical labels that clearly describe the given form of solitary activity, I have exercised a bit of conceptual license with certain parts of speech. Thus, peripatetics and reflexives appear here as nouns rather than adjectives. In addition, I refer to engrossments as a back formation from the verb to engross. The fourth category, regimens, has always been a noun, of course. However, as I shall indicate later on, my definition expands to include a broader range of activities than everyday usage ordinarily suggests.

Peripatetics

Wandering, browsing, and skimming seldom count as notable traits in sociological analysis of human behavior. We prefer to think that our actions, our solitary conduct and interpersonal conduct alike, have some sort of logical from or narrative continuity. So deep-seated is this disposition that to describe an action as wandering, or, in idiomatic terms as "all over the map," implies a degree of disorganization bordering on incoherence. From this point of view, the more behavior wanders the less sense it makes. Moreover, to describe an individual as wandering has negative connotations of its own implying that he or she may be confused, intoxicated, or, in extreme situations, mentally deranged. While many forms of conduct obviously do unfold in logically or narratively well-structured ways, and while a person whose wandering behavior truly doesn't make sense is a legitimate source of concern, our broad disposition to view all forms of loosely structured behavior in this way leaves in the dark a broad range of commonplace and perfectly sane forms of conduct that are familiar features of everyday life. These forms of conduct unfold via oblique moves and create elliptical patterns. Like tourists upon arrival in a new town, their paths circle, twist, turn one way and then another, without any particular place to go, slowing or stopping when they encounter something interesting, then moving on again at a faster pace. True, our tourists may have nicely integrated episodes as they come across a civic landmark or a local shop. Still, their walk as a whole is a disorganized affair. I call such loose-jointed wanderings peripatetics. In terms of the classification of solitary action shown in Figure 4.1, they are loosely structured forms of conduct on the one hand, and only intermittently (hence only weakly) engaging or absorbing on the other. Though my concern here is with solitary peripatetics, the peripatetic nature of interpersonal behavior is so common yet disattended that a brief digression is in order to establish the unexceptional nature in everyday life at large.

Consider casual conversation, which is not necessarily well known in most sociological circles for its oblique moves and circuitous paths. However, ethnomethodologists are a notable exception in this regard, and one of Harold Garfinkel's early and best-known investigations from *Studies in Ethnomethodology* provides an exceptionally clear example of the peripatetic nature of casual conversation. The passage below is excerpted from a longer conversation that Garfinkel uses to illustrate the "documentary method," by which he means the ways in which details situated in an unfolding conversational context implicitly reference other items not necessarily referenced anywhere in the conversation that are mutually understood by conversationalists and therefore can figure in the talk without being explicitly said. However, my concern at the moment is not with the documentary method per se. Instead, I wish to draw attention to how the conversation wanders from one topic to the next without any tight narrative or logical connections. As the excerpt I have selected from the conversation begins, a husband and wife discuss the husband's recent shopping trip with their young son, Dana (Garfinkel, 1967, pp. 38–39).

> HUSBAND: Dana succeeded in putting a penny in a parking meter today without being picked up.
> WIFE: Did you take him to the record store?
> HUSBAND: No, to the shoe repair shop.
> WIFE: What for?
> HUSBAND: I got some new shoelaces for my shoes.
> WIFE: Your loafers need mending too.

Notice how the theme changes peripatetically here. The husband's mention of Dana's accomplishment might reasonably continue with more discussion about the boy. Instead (making an inference via the documentary method) the wife jumps peripatetically to a question about a stop at the record store during the shopping trip the husband took with their son. In a better-connected move, the husband indicates he did not go to the record store but rather to the shoe repair shop. The wife quite logically asks about the reason for this stop and the husband quite logically says he purchased some shoelaces. But then the wife makes an oblique move as she mentions that the husband's loafers need to be repaired. Overall, there is no straightforward or implicit path being marked out even in the small bit of conversation. Though each step makes sense in some context, there is no teleology from the husband's first remark to the wife's last. After all, the fact that Dana put a penny in a parking meter has nothing whatsoever to do with the fact that the husband's shoes need to be repaired. This is, in short, a peripatetic conversation.[2] This is not to say that all conversations are equally peripatetic. However, many informal conversations, not only between domestic partners, but between friends, colleagues, and, in a kind of apotheosis of conversational peripatetics, among mingling guests at cocktail parties, zigzag and meander without ever really going anywhere.

Now to return to solitary action: if conversations often wander peripatetically, we can expect to find a similar tendency among forms of conduct performed by solitary individuals as well. Indeed, it is easier to make loose-jointed transitions from one move to the next when one is disengaged from others. After all, when a person is on her own she need not attend to a mutually produced context of interaction as it unfolds, nor does she have any normative obligation to politely attend to others. The individual is only accountable to herself for taking tangents, circling in and out of various focal points, or jumping forward (laterally) from one sequence of locally produced order to the next. Of course, as will become evident when discussion turns to regimens and engrossments, the absence of conversational restraints

2. Garfinkel himself is aware of the peripatetic qualities of social activities. This insight is best developed in his essay "The Rational Properties of Scientific and Common-Sense Activities," (1967, pp. 262–283).

by no means makes it inevitable that all forms of solitary conduct must develop in a peripatetic form. However, it should cause no surprise to find a sizable group of activities classified as peripatetics within the solitary domain.

What kinds of solitary peripatetics are we talking about? How do they proceed? Consider as an example: a type of casual wandering practiced in modern everyday life, the meandering excursion of the urban flâneur on the lookout for whatever crosses her path as she strolls through the byways and thoroughfares of the city. Charting an aimless path on a weekday afternoon, let us say our flâneur encounters an unusual scene; the traffic lights have failed at one of the busiest intersections in the area. Almost immediately, cars clog the intersection and traffic from all directions comes to a halt and backs up as horns blare and a few drivers begin to shout. Then, two volunteers jump into the intersection, each intent upon coordinating the traffic. For a moment the two would-be traffic cops contradict one another and drivers ignore them both. Then, one volunteer steps aside and the other takes control, and with some hand gestures and body motions manages to unjam the intersection and coordinate the flow of traffic, which now travels freely again. Soon police and workers arrive and repair the traffic light. A few minutes later all parties involved have dispersed, the intersection looks as if nothing had happened, and the flâneur, who had been paying rapt attention as the incident played out, now moves along in search of another interesting scene.

This episode—brief, self-contained, yet fully absorbing to the flâneur for as long as it lasts—is the sort of incident that makes what seems to be a pointless trip into a set of intermittently fascinating urban vignettes. The episode also usefully illustrates several basic features of solitary peripatetics. For one thing, there is the aimless path. Notice also that the episode of interest is preceded and followed by portions of the walk during which nothing special or unusual catches the individual's eye. This pattern of intermittent involvement is common to many solitary peripatetics, which is to say that many solitary peripatetics are patchworks of self-contained, unfolding sequences that hold the individual's attention, along with sequences that offer nothing absorbing to hold the individual at all.

This pattern turns up in other perambulations such as nature walks on beaches or in the woods and in some very different kinds of routines as well. Consider the way we read newspapers and magazines, hopscotching the headlines, features, pictures, and ads until something catches our eye and we pause to give it a closer look. Consider also how we shop, not so much when we target a small list of items in advance and stick to the list in the store, but rather when we survey the bins, racks, and counters for whatever items happen to strike our fancy or be on sale. Shopping in this way bears a surprising resemblance to the way people used to (and many still do) wander the open stacks in the library, pausing to sample a bit of one book here and another book there, and collecting a few that we will borrow to read in earnest at home. Of course, today hundreds of millions of people surf the web,[3] and even greater numbers surf channels quickly and aimlessly with

3. By surfing the web I refer specifically to sequences in which an individual proceeds from one link to the next without seeking a specific web page or web address. Thus, searching Wikipedia or a dictionary site for a single item is not defined here as web surfing. Performing broader searches, such as for medical information or for comparative prices on a product for sale, also does not qualify as web surfing under the present definition. However, following various links on a broader search, such as high school students considering applications to a wide range of colleges or movie fans searching for the latest news from Hollywood, qualifies as surfing because there is no logical path or pattern to chart a course between moves. In the same sense, going directly to a friend's Facebook site should not be regarded as surfing, while skimming titles on a chat board or message board falls within the definition.

their television remotes or scan stations on car radios in search of favorite songs, news, weather, and traffic reports. Here again, in the electronic media we find activities that share the pattern of scanning, focusing, and then scanning again, that characterize the wanderings of the urban flâneur. And the list of solitary peripatetics is far from complete. Certain industries employ inspectors whose job it is to scan production lines for the oddly shaped or poorly prepared item that differs from the far greater number of products that do not stand out in any way at all. Then too, to cite a favorite peripatetic of mine, each evening countless individuals casually survey refrigerators and pantry shelves in search of whatever they may find to prepare a late-night snack.

Peripatetics as Solitary Action

Since peripatetics are the weakest and most loosely structured form of solitary action, two questions seem worthy of expanded consideration. First, why should we consider as forms of solitary action open-ended activities that boil down to skimming, browsing, and otherwise wandering in search of whatever may attract our attention along the way? Second, how do we make sense of the distinctive subset of peripatetics that can be performed purely within the mind that I term *mental peripatetics*, such as daydreaming, reminiscing, and imagining? Here again the question ultimately turns on issues regarding the nature of solitary action. In the present section I shall explain why it makes sense to regard peripatetics as, in general, a form of action. However, the status of mental peripatetics in particular is not so clear. In the next section I will explain why mental peripatetics qualify as solitary action in some respects but not in others.

One elementary fact about peripatetics as solitary action seems beyond dispute, namely that they are agentic forms of conduct, that is, behavior that the individual in some way controls.

Anything more to be said about peripatetics as a form of action hinges on how the essentially contested concept of action is to be defined. My view, as developed in chapter 3, is that to qualify as action a behavior must be performed via socially acquired skills. Thus, the automatic blinks that result when an object comes in close proximity to one's eyes does not qualify as an action, while the scanning movements of eyes when reading is a solitary practice since the skills involved are acquired through socialization. To say the same thing in other words, all activities that count as actions are indigenous to the ways of life of a historically situated cultural group. If we accept this definition then it seems quite reasonable to include peripatetics as a general type of solitary action, no more or less agentic, socially acquired, or culturally specific than other forms.

Consider the kind of reading that is common to many peripatetic activities today. Peripatetics involving newspapers, magazines, and web surfing, among others, require more than basic literacy. All of these peripatetics require the rapid and efficient skimming or browsing of topically distinct and spatially separated items (e.g., headlines, website titles, and links to others pages). Today we take these specialized reading skills for granted as if they were as old as literacy itself. But the history of reading suggests otherwise. According to Alberto Manguel in *A History of Reading* (1997, pp. 46–50), until well into the Middle Ages, reading material was composed in continuous blocks of script, lacking punctuation and any spatial division between words. This type of text required reading practices that modern cultures have forgotten or regard as obsolete.[4] However, since pre-modern texts provided few opportunities for readers to move quickly from one

4. Manguel also notes that this early mode of composition was designed in concert with reading out loud, which was a common practice among solitary (but not silent) readers, as well as those who read to others in groups.

item to another, it is hard to imagine browsing or skimming as a standardized cultural practice. Peripatetic reading is thus a historically and culturally delimited form of solitary conduct.

Like human activities at large, every peripatetic activity has a history of its own with culturally specific practices and skills. In many cultural groups, up to and including small towns in Europe and North America, no more than half a century ago shopping was an interactive way of life with its own conversational rituals and routines. Customers seldom browsed the goods in market stalls or small shops for very long by themselves. Even if they shopped unaccompanied by others, they would eventually encounter merchants who made small talk with customers, many of whom were acquainted with these merchants from various community organizations. Today, in our ever-larger supermarkets and discount department stores, many customers browse the aisles on their own, unaccompanied by others, and with no personal contact with merchants. Shopping in these stores is now either a targeted search for necessary things or a peripatetic trip through the aisles searching for bargains, new products, or whatever they happen to come across that seems to fill a need (even if they had no intention to fill that need on the way into the store). This kind of solitary peripatetic shopping is of more recent vintage than we may think and comes with its own set of skills (e.g., comparing labels and prices) and is a far cry from functionally analogous practices in the United States or Europe in, say, 1930. However, lest it appear that peripatetics are unique to the last fifty years, while some peripatetics have only arisen recently, others involve skills that are rarely practiced today. Thus, whatever small percentage of people in modern cultures know how to forage for food on uncultivated lands, it was a ubiquitous way of life among natives in hunting and gathering tribes. The same point applies to pre-modern navigation techniques and other skills that members of such tribes would need to survive when voyaging out alone beyond their familiar paths.

As previously noted, there is nothing uniquely solitary about peripatetic behavior. Conversational exchanges unfold with the same lack of logical or narrative teleology as any solitary peripatetic one cares to name. However, because conversation is a collaborative activity, each move in a conversation must be secured in a mutually produced context. Therefore, to make the leap comprehensible to all parties concerned, when a speaker abruptly changes the topic of conversation she relies on implicit allusions to background knowledge and expectations shared by others in the conversation group. Here we arrive at a point where solitary peripatetics part company with conversation. The solitary individual engaged in peripatetics has no reason to coordinate contextual development with others. When it comes to context formation, things must still make sense, but only in terms of how the individual makes sense of her own moves. The question thus arises as to how solitary peripatetics remain contextualized at all. Is a wanderer truly free to chart her own course at random, bouncing here and there like an astronaut freed from the earth's gravity? Or do contexts still shape and channel how she proceeds, as is true for peripatetic interactions? Since de-contextual behavior within the bound of society is as unlikely as weightless movements here on earth, sociological intuition tells us that even the most footloose ramble through city streets or the most loose-jointed session of jumping from one website to the next must be intrinsically structured, at least in part, by various characteristics of the local environment. But then the question reemerges in a more refined form: If solitary peripatetic behaviors include elliptical shifts and oblique connections as the individual moves from one item to the next, how does structure enter into this pattern of wandering moves at all? In brief, how do the local environments shape loose-jointed activities? Two useful answers present themselves: one in terms of the meshing of skills and background knowledge, the other in terms of available options. Each tells us something about context formation as an intrinsic aspect of solitary peripatetics.

Solitary individuals engaged in peripatetic activity may have no need to coordinate their moves with others via allusions to mutually shared background information. Nevertheless, they still need sufficient background information to mesh relevant skills with background knowledge in a given milieu. The meshing of skills and knowledge in a milieu for any given solitary peripatetic requires some socialization. For example, well-socialized library patrons generally know how to use a library catalog and how to read maps keyed to catalog numbers to find their way to materials of interest. When a patron locates an item she may also have certain background expectations that other books of interest may be shelved in the vicinity, and thus a session of open-ended browsing may ensue that ultimately may carry the patron to unanticipated books and unexpected subject matter. In brief, the skilled patron knows and expects that she will find more than she is looking for. Every peripatetic has its own meshing skills and background knowledge within a given milieu. This is why, though the nature walker and the urban flâneur both wander about looking for appealing things to observe, they are still doing very different things. The nature walker knows how to spot and expects to find flora, fauna, and striking natural tableaux, while the flâneur knows how to spot and expects to find the charming or unusual urban scene. Their diverse forms of background knowledge are only relevant in specific settings, and by the same token, the setting only becomes an environment for peripatetic activity through the exercise of their skills.

The local environment of a solitary peripatetic does more than enable a skillful individual to engage in a particular form of peripatetic conduct. It also presents a range of possible options. A public library offers patrons recent novels, popular biographies, do-it-yourself guides and so on. Academic libraries offer patrons specialized monographs, edited collections of research reports, and books of many kinds that are now out of print. The casual browser in the stacks of either library is unlikely to come across many of the holdings in the other. The same holds true for all peripatetics. But the environments of peripatetics must allow sufficient range for wandering to occur. One cannot easily wander very long in small racks of paperbacks in a newsstand. One needs enough options to serendipitously encounter a variety of different things. Thus, a public library patron may set out to find a book about Ervin "Magic" Johnson, the legendary member of the Basketball Hall of Fame. But while she is in close proximity (i.e., the shelf with books on others named "Johnson" in the biography section), she may discover an intriguing biography of Lyndon Baines Johnson, the thirty-sixth president of the United States. Of course, there can be too many options as well. Browsing the web offers an instructive example. Now that the web provides more sites than the individual can visit in a reasonable period of time (most of which come with multiple pages and hundreds of individual links), the peripatetic web surfer would almost certainly be overwhelmed by available options were it not for Google and other search engines. A search engine, in a sense, is a device that creates manageable sets of options. Some searches, of course, are targeted for a single link or bit of information. However, Google also sets limits for the casual surfer. Thus, a person may perform a search on British movies stars or northern Italian cuisine and instantly the search engines provide a limited list of entries: a temporary, specialized, peripatetic environment.

In the meshing of skills and environments, the structuring of solitary peripatetics always leaves open a field of options through which no particular path or pattern of moves is required, prescribed, or recommended. This loose structuration, in turn, raises concerns about the capacity of items within the open field of options to attract and hold attention. However, what makes peripatetics a weak form of behavior is that it is in the nature of browsing, skimming, scanning, and so on that even the most appealing items individuals may encounter as they proceed will keep them occupied for only a limited period of time. When reading a magazine, for example, readers may be attracted by a headline or a picture and settle in to read the associated story or report. However, given that magazines are organized to offer an eclectic compendium of items rather than a homogeneous series of pieces on similar themes, when readers complete one article, their attention is released and they return to skimming headlines. Something similar often happens when channel-hopping with a television remote. Though there is an ever-present possibility that a truly engrossing program may turn up, channel-hoppers often sample a scene, a few sports scores, a news report, a recipe, or a few scenes from a drama before losing interest and moving on. In this sense, items available for peripatetic browsing are like blossoms available to pollinating insects, such as bees. Just as any given blossom attracts a bee for only a short period of time, so any item in a peripatetic field has a limited appeal to keep a wandering individual engaged.

So how then does the wandering individual chart a finite course through a peripatetic field? Here, as in all issues in the sociology of action, we inevitably reach a level of individual differences based on psychology, biography, and even day-to-day variations in the life of the subject that admits no generalization at all.[5] Nevertheless, some degree of generalization can be made

5. As many ethnomethodological studies of individual interactions suggest, this level of individuality is reached in interaction as well.

about matters of choice in peripatetic fields so long as our level of analysis remains above the level of personal preference. As Eviatar Zerubavel (1997, p. 33–34 passim) observes in his account of the sociological foundations of cognition, the things we focus on (e.g., our interests and tastes) are shaped, at least in part, by the cultural frames we acquire as socialized members of a particular group (which Zerubavel defines as "optical communities").[6] Thus, when teenagers find a song they like while scanning a car radio, the song's appeal very likely was shaped to a certain extent by tastes (e.g., for certain artists or genres) they share with their friends.

Mental Peripatetics

Until now the peripatetic milieu at issue required individuals to wander through a material or media environment located beyond their own minds. Even the digitized web link can only be reached by entering information via some sort of computer hardware (e.g., keyboard, mouse, monitor, etc.). But we need not move beyond ourselves in any way whatsoever to engage in some kinds of peripatetic behavior. All we need to do is produce loose-jointed connections between symbolically and emotionally fraught images generated in our own minds. Such mental

6. Advertising and marketing research would be ineffective in the absence of culturally shared foci of attention. One result of such research is that many items are designed to catch the attention of as many browsing individuals as possible. Thus, culturally salient symbols and themes are deployed in clever ways to interest the largest possible number of readers skimming ads in periodicals and websites. Packaging and displays of merchandise in retail settings do much the same. Even the book jackets from commercial publishers are designed as much out of concern to catch the interest of as many browsing readers as possible. Of course, advertising and marketing cannot reach every individual. Nor can they sell overpriced or inferior products for any extended period of time. Nonetheless, the fact that they are effective at all demonstrates that cultural preferences have some degree of influence in shaping items of interest to peripatetic browsers.

peripatetics include daydreaming, fantasizing, reminiscing, and wishful thinking, along with their less reputable siblings: fearful, spiteful, and sinful thinking. Ironically, given his dim view of the prevalence of solitary conduct discussed in chapter 2, Erving Goffman had a keen awareness of these mental peripatetics:

> It is known, although perhaps not sufficiently appreciated, that the individual spends a considerable amount of time bathing his wounds in fantasy, imagining the worst things that might befall him, daydreaming about matters sexual, monetary, and so forth. He also rehearses what he will say when the time comes, and privately formulates what he should have said after it has come and gone. Not being able to get others to speak the lines he wanted to hear from them he scripts and commands these performances on the small stage in his head (Goffman, 1974, p. 551).

Goffman's survey illustrates the prevalence of mental peripatetics in everyday life, but Goffman abbreviates the variety of mental wanderings and his closing dramaturgical metaphor leaves central questions unanswered. In terms of variety, Goffman surely is right to underscore the numerous flights of imagination that keep the self at the center of the individual's interest and attention from beginning to end. Though we can speculate on whether imaginings and daydreams in cultures less individualistic than our own would circle around the concerns of the self to an equal extent, even within our own culture there is no reason to believe that mental wandering is strictly confined to the self. Who among us has not envisioned frightening possibilities when we unexpectedly lose contact with a loved one or mentally imagined a loved one's good news even though the events in question have yet to occur? Nor do our mental peripatetics necessarily feature people at all. Some of us daydream about places we have yet to see or reminisce about places we saw long ago. Sports fans chart plans to glory for their favorite teams and film buffs create mental montages from memories of films they last watched many years ago. People envision prospects for war and peace, social progress, and treatments for incurable diseases.[7] To give Goffman his due, it is fair to say that at least in the individualistic social climates in the modern Western world, a kind of cultural, centripetal force draws even far-flung mental wanderings back to the self.

However, Goffman provides little help of any kind when it comes to the question of how mental peripatetics unfold. There is something facile and unpersuasive in Goffman's dramaturgical imagery of the individual as playwright and director of performances in her own mind. But the question is how, given our obvious inability to directly observe the flow of images in one another's minds, can we obtain a more convincing account than Goffman provides of the way in which the peripatetic mind unfolds its images? Methodologists of the social sciences have wrestled futilely with similar questions from the dawn of the various disciplines. However, the most persuasive accounts often come from the works of fiction by writers gifted with the ability to translate the mercurial emergence of mental images into vivid yet unsettled prose on the page. Many readers agree that no one has captured the elliptical movements of the wandering mind better than Marcel Proust. Proust's extraordinary "madeleine episode" in the first volume (*Swann's Way*) of his *In Search of Lost Time* provides a remarkably precise (and notably beautiful) account of a single sequence of mental peripatetics from which we learn a

7. John Lennon's lyrics to "Imagine" suggest that some people fantasize about utopian societies, though such fantasies may have been more prevalent in the 1960s than they are today.

great deal. Proust's "madeleine episode," told from the narrator's point of view, provides an account of the images that the narrator recalls from the stimulus provided by a bite from a madeleine (small cookie or cake) accompanied by a sip of tea. The episode begins when the vaguely melancholy narrator takes his first bite. Immediately he feels an intense but indefinite sense of pleasure and joy. He commences a concerted search through his memories for the origin of these rare feelings. When his efforts fail he decides to abandon the attempt. Then, just as he turns away, his mind spontaneously comes alive, whereupon he instantly visualizes a series of lucid and evocative images from the past.

> And suddenly the memory revealed itself. The taste was that of the little piece of madeleine which on Sunday mornings at Combray (because, on those mornings I did not go out before mass), when I went to say good morning to her in her bedroom, my aunt Leonie used to give me, dipping it first in her own cup of tea or tisane (Proust [1913] 1992, p. 63).

This single memory immediately bursts and transforms into a cluster of childhood impressions far beyond the cookie he tasted on Sunday mornings with his aunt.

> And as soon as I had recognized the taste of the Madeleine . . . immediately the old grey house upon the street, where [his aunt's] room was, rose up like a stage set to attach itself to the little pavilion opening onto the garden which had been built out behind it for my parents . . . and with the house in town, from morning to night and in all weather, the Square where I used to be sent before lunch, the streets along which I used to run errands, the country roads we took when it was fine (p. 64).

Proust's madeleine episode describes only a single sequence of reminiscence. Nevertheless, while it may be more nostalgic than other mental peripatetics, it provides a valuable window into how mental wanderings take shape. The wandering itself is plain to see. The narrator's memories begin on Sunday mornings in his aunt's bedroom and end with a rapid-fire sequence of vivid images of locales in the town and things he did in those settings as a boy. Well before Goffman, Proust's narrator compares these remembrances of his hometown to a scene on a stage. As with Goffman, this metaphor is not a good fit. A stage set confines scenes to a particular place. But the narrator's memories skip from the pavilion behind his house to the town square, through the streets where he ran errands, to the country roads where he walked with his parents. If a metaphor is in order for his youthful impressions of his hometown (anachronistic though it may be), the reminiscence might be said to resemble a montage of nostalgic video clips playing almost simultaneously on the narrator's inner mental screen.

Metaphors offer little insight into a basic matter of sociological interest with regard to Proust's account of the sequences of his narrator's memories or for mental peripatetics in general. The question is: Are we dealing with a form of action here? Does an individual actually produce a string of images when his memory or imagination spins a loosely connected series of scenes and impressions? My equivocal answer is yes on some counts, but no on others. Specifically: yes, mental peripatetics are social in the sense that all unique and personal references notwithstanding, they involve culturally shaped images. But no, these mental wanderings markedly differ from what sociology and the general public alike understands by action because the individual exercises no agency as the mental wandering proceeds. Let me clarify both the positive and negative sides of this answer.

Cultural imagery of items, gestures, ways of life, relationships, and so on that members of a given social group easily recognize as one thing rather than another in their everyday lives shapes every recollected item in a reminiscence in a collectively defined way (cf. Zerubavel, 1997, p. 3.). Proust's narrator had to be familiar with the lifestyles, architecture, street life, and other aspects as culturally defined, not only in his own town but in small towns more generally in his region of late nineteenth-century France. Of course he recalls personal details rather than generic images. However, memories are not certifiable truths. In some measure, we imagine what we recall (cf. Proust [1913] 1992, p. 61). To a certain degree, what we imagine is autobiographical as well. The point to notice here is that beyond creative recollection that includes autobiographical feelings and thoughts, what we recall are elements of what Zerubavel (1997, p. 81) calls "remembrance environments," items embedded in the common milieu we at one time shared with members of our family, communities, work groups, and other collectivities. This point is not confined to memories, of course. When we imagine the words (the apology, the thank you, the praise) in our minds that we wish we had said, as Goffman suggests in his gloss on mental peripatetics, the very speech acts we envision are in some measure matters of social convention. After all, the gestures by which an apology is rendered in one local milieu may differ substantially from the gestures of apology in another. When the mind wanders, it has no pan-historical or trans-cultural set of images on which to draw. Mental peripatetics are always personal to some extent, but the personal is always indigenous to or situated within ways of life shared with others. And it is in this sense that mental peripatetics are social.

If mental peripatetics are social, are they also forms of action as well? Though sociologists are inclined to lump all behavior as action, this is not the case here. In order to clarify this point in the broadest possible terms I shall refer to an aspect of action that is an elementary common denominator of sociological concepts of action, including not only the concept of solitary action I developed in chapter 3, but a host of others including concepts explicitly or implicitly embedded in the works of George Herbert Mead, Erving Goffman, Harold Garfinkel, and Anthony Giddens. That common denominator is agency. In its most elemental sense, the presence or absence of agency in human behavior boils down to a basic question: To what degree is the behavior in question under the individual's control? So inclusive is agency that it can admit tacit behavior of which the individual is only dimly aware. Thus, to take a simple tacit behavior, humming a few random notes counts as action because the individual can pause, resume, or cease the humming at any time even though she or he may pay little attention to the humming so long as there is no interruption.[8] The advantage of using this extremely relaxed sense of agency as a criterion for action here is that it adds weight to a conclusion that any given form of activity, in this case mental peripatetics, falls beyond the conceptual ambit of action.

Presuming agency in this sense as the criterion for action, there is reason to doubt that individuals exercise any agency in the images brought together by their wandering minds during mental peripatetics. Return for a moment to Proust's madeleine scene. Notice that the narrator's memories begin to flow only after he suspends his focused search for the images associated with the joy he feels upon tasting the madeleine and thereby allows his mind to relax. Relaxation (or release) rather than control sets

---

8. Humming in this sense is a diversion, a form of undemanding behavior that requires less attention than the main task at hand. There will be more to say about diversions in a later section of this chapter.

his memories in motion.[9] Notice too that his memories appear to him at a remarkable speed. Individuals cannot control images that materialize this rapidly. When the body is engaged in wandering, even if it involves nothing more than the eye scanning a printed page, activity moves no faster than the body's physiological capabilities. Another kind of braking slows us down when we concentrate to think in a focused way. Hence, as the mind bears down it slows the images so that they can be manipulated at a manageable pace (see more on this in chapter 5). It is hard to deny that mental peripatetics are an activity of some kind. The mind, after all, is putting images together in a selective way. Still, in the absence of agentic control, the individual is not exercising agency in any conventional sense of the term.

REGIMENS

What do all of the following varieties of action share in common: washing dishes, working in noisy factories, practicing drills when learning new skills, and driving motor vehicles alone in smooth flowing traffic over standardized expressways or familiar local routes? Consider three similarities between all of the above. First, all of these actions often are performed by solitary individuals. Second, there is only one correct way to apply the skills implicated in the way each of these activities is performed. For example: the steering, braking, and accelerating involved in driving a truck or a car admits little room for error; practicing math skills or musical scales counts every error as a correctable mistake.

9. The madeleine episode has inspired psychological investigations of "involuntary memory." For a collection of essays and research reports see Mace (2007). The point I make here expands the notion of involuntary mental activity to include mental peripatetics at large.

Third, the most well-known similarity between these activities is that they have well-deserved reputations for inducing boredom. Though occasional exceptions may be found,[10] in general these activities are chores at best, barely endurable drudgery at worst.

I call the category of solitary actions that includes these examples *regimens*.[11] In terms of the two axes in Figure 4.1, regimens are characterized by tight structuration of standardized practices and a weak capacity to engage actors in the performance of the action at hand. Now, the structuration of regimens is easily understood. This analytical trait is present when the practices that compose a sequence of action are required, which is to say that these practices must be performed in a prescribed way. Notice two subsidiary points about the tight structuration of regimens here. First, it is the proper performance of practices rather than the chains or sequences of action that are tightly structured. This may seem like a trivial distinction until we take into account forms of behavior such as driving a motor vehicle in which the sequencing of practices may vary with local conditions (e.g., drivers may accelerate to pass slow moving traffic or brake when taking an expressway exit). Accelerating and braking must be performed in the proper way (e.g., with just the right amount of foot pressure on the proper pedal). Even very small deviations from proper form can result in great harm. Of course some regimens such as factory work or clerical office work may

10. The compulsive work ethic that Max Weber ([1904–05] 1958) identifies as the Spirit of Capitalism may be a historical exception as well in that individuals imbued with the Spirit ideal typically may enjoy the rigors of regimented work. However, this presumes that sufficient work calms the anxieties and self-doubt that produces the compulsion in the first place.

11. In common usage the term regimen often describes a course of action prescribed so that when strictly followed, individuals will recover from an illness or otherwise improve their health. However, from a broader view the term regimen simply refers to any course of action that an individual strictly follows.

include entire sequences of practices that must be performed in the proper order or the employee is likely to hear from his or her supervisor. However, the emphasis on the tight structuration of regimens does not insist upon mandatory sequence.

Second, this definition of regimen leaves latitude for both voluntary actions and obedient compliance with directives from others. In fact, as Erving Goffman (1983) might say, the performance of regimens is generally a "mixed[-]motive game." On the one hand, even music students who practice scales because of their earnest intent to master an instrument must follow drills assigned by others. On the other hand, even assembly line workers with no love whatsoever for the rigid requirements of their work may return to the factory each day without complaint out of a sense of dignity and self-respect for fulfilling their personal and familial responsibilities (see Lamont 2000). This is not to say that assembly line work is intrinsically rewarding. Such work is still alienating in the classical Marxian sense, that is, production processes are dictated on the one hand by operations designed to yield a profit and on the other hand by the demands of the industrial technology employed. The main point, however, is that regimens make performance demands on the individual regardless of what her motives for correct performance may be.

Regimens may be tightly structured, but that does not account for their second analytical trait, which is that these solitary activities fail to engage the actor's attention. Adjectives like dull, boring, tedious, mind-numbing, and so on are commonly associated with regimens such as office work, factory work, and school assignments to such an extent that those descriptors may be unspoken yet implicitly understood. What makes regimens so boring and dull? It can't be the tight structuration per se. After all, as we saw in chapter 3, and as we will consider in greater detail when discussion turns to engrossments later on in this chapter, there are games such as solitaire that are as tightly structured as, say, driving a car, but which capture and involve the player in a rather impressive way. Bear in mind how tightly structured solitaire is. The player has no control over the rules or the cards dealt and must make every move correctly to have a good chance to win. This is not very different than the degree of conformity expected of the office worker entering information into a database or a factory worker who solders connections on an assembly line. So why are regimens so uninvolving? The answer is that they lack any ongoing formation of context. Assembly line work epitomizes the point in an especially vivid way. An iPad rolls into a workstation on an assembly line, a worker solders a certain set of connections, the iPad moves on and another takes its place. While the procedure goes on all day long, the context never changes. Assembly lines are hardly unique. Consider another example. A student is assigned the following list of a dozen spelling words to memorize: taught, taut, thought, thou, threw, through, throw, thrive, trap, tray, trounce, trousers. Though it would be a cruel teacher who would assign so many similar sounding words (and the definitions that ultimately distinguish them), the homonyms and alliterations in the list emphasize the dull, tedious nature of the work. There is no way to develop an unfolding context from the list. The only thing that connects these words is that some of them sound alike. The words tell no story, they do not follow a logical progression, nor can they be arranged in a meaningful sentence. In brief, the spelling list, like the assembly line, is nothing more than a set of practices that (for whatever reasons) simply must be done.

Though there is no substantive context that can be developed in learning these spelling words, there is one formal technique the student may use to produce a kind of thin, virtual progression, and this technique has analogs in many other regimens as well. The technique is simple. Since the list includes a dozen words, the student may simply subtract each word from the total after she is confident she has mastered it. Though the list still does not unfold with an involving context, she has introduced a metric that enables her to gauge how much of her task she has completed and how much of it remains undone. The use of formal metrics to create a context where none would otherwise exist is quite common. In addition to using the number of tasks that are completed or remain, other metrics employ space and time. For example, motorists may use mileage or elapsed time to determine how close they are to the end of a long trip. When mowing my lawn, I complete the work in sections in order to gauge my progress. No doubt, agricultural workers do the same when working in the fields. In factories and offices, time is not only a metric for wages earned, but for the progress of the workday as well. Though we take it for granted, there is something remarkable about how effectively synchronized solitary workers are at the end of the day. Whereas a few minutes before closing time cubicles and offices may be filled with office workers, each one at work on a solitary and regimented task, a few minutes later the workstations are as empty as if their inhabitants had responded to a circadian cue.[12]

Coping with Regimens: Patience and Discipline
The rich, if they like, may pay others to attend to many of their dull, solitary chores; for the rest of us those chores are impossible to avoid. Here we arrive at a seldom-asked question: How do people cope with the sheer drudgery of unengaging tasks, tasks

---

12. For a broader ranging analysis of time as a metric see Zerubavel (1981).

that neither develop any kind of context nor provide any intrinsic satisfaction of their own? Like many questions in the sociology of action, there is no one-size-fits-all answer here. Indeed, it seems reasonable to propose three different means of coping with different kinds of regimens: (1) patience, (2) diversions, and (3) discipline. These methods are not alternatives. To the contrary, as I now want to suggest, each works only for regimens of a particular kind.

Patience is the essential and most successful coping strategy, but since it can only be applied in limited situations I shall discuss it only briefly here. The limiting condition is that patience staves off boredom only when regimens are easy and they can be completed in short order. For example, raking leaves off a lawn may be an unengaging task, but the work makes few demands and it usually just takes a few hours once or twice a year. Of course, the effectiveness of patience declines as the demands of the work increase. Patience may be all that most people need to cope with completing application forms or infrequent chores. Merely knowing that the task need not be repeated generally suffices to enable individuals to ignore the tedious nature of the work and get the job done. Still, patience with regimens is never anything more than a temporary fix. The challenges of coping intensify when regimens must be repeated as part of the ordinary routines of everyday life, colloquially dubbed "the daily grind," a term that recognizes that such regimens are difficult to bear. Coping strategies for recurrent regimens fall into two categories, diversions and disciplines, depending on the kinds of tasks at hand.

Consider recurrent but less-demanding regimens. Though some physical labor may be involved, these tasks do not deplete the individual's energy or strength. Many, but not all mechanical factory routines fall under this heading,[13] as do many kinds of mechanized domestic work. These regimens also make few cognitive demands. This cognitive simplicity enables the individual to perform such tasks as repetitive routines. And in turn, unthinkingly performed tasks leave some cognitive resources available for actors to divert some attention to other things.

Like flavoring that makes unpalatable medicines easier to swallow, diversions distract attention from the monotony of undemanding regimens. But unlike medicinal flavorings, diversions from simple regimens often seem inconspicuous from a bystander's point of view. Diversions grow more impressive when we recognize how ubiquitous they are. Actually, the most ubiquitous diversions are heard rather than seen. Consider the sound systems found in reach of the driver's seat in every enclosed motor vehicle regardless of size, function, price, or design. Why are they there? Undoubtedly, one reason is to give the large number of solitary drivers a diversion from the dullness of the road.[14] Audio entertainment is also commonly found in a wide range of other venues where people perform undemanding tasks. Soft, steady streams of music; talk; news; and sports can be heard at workbenches and most other sites where individuals work on

13. I refer here to solitary assembly line work. Sociological studies seldom note that the sheer noisy tumult of factory machinery often precludes substantive interaction on the factory floor. As this quote from an interview by Studs Terkel (1972, p. 160) suggests, factory noise often enforces workday solitude.

The noise, oh it's tremendous. You open your mouth and you're liable to get a mouthful of sparks . . . you don't compete against the noise. You go to yell and at the same time you're straining to maneuver the gun to where you have to weld.

14. A recent figure cited by Emma Rothschild (2009) indicates that 76% of Americans who drive to work do so by themselves. Over the past few decades the mobile telephone has become available to most drivers as well. However, while we tend to notice motorists using their phones (especially after they make dangerous moves), we do not equally notice the preponderance of solitary drivers who are not so engaged. One thing is certain: sound systems remain standard features on almost all motor vehicles.

their own.[15] Since the advent of miniaturized earphones, which began with the Sony Walkman in the 1980s, it has become common to find people engaged in unchallenging tasks who, isolated from any aural interruptions, are in a sound world all to themselves. Diversions are not limited to audio programming, of course. Snacking, for example, is a popular diversion as well. The broad range of foods sold by retailers on busy highways share only one thing in common: all of them are designed and packaged so that they can be conveniently consumed. The items themselves are designed for easy manipulation (e.g., miniature cookies, bite-sized pretzels), and the packages afford easy access for drivers who presumably have only one hand to spare (e.g., wide-mouthed boxes and bags). And diversions for drivers work the same way for workers as well. We need look no further than the ubiquitous vending machines, entirely filled with conveniently packaged servings, for one to find evidence that a good deal of solitary snacking is going on. And yet let's not forget domestic diversions. The homemaker cleaning house after the kids have gone to school is just as likely as the factory or office worker to be accompanied by the sound of the radio (or the speaker from a television set) and to have easily portable snacks on hand. Finally, diversions are hardly confined to interior spaces. Consider outdoor diversions such as street foods, billboards, and retail goods on sidewalk display. Then too, pedestrians through the ages have been known to whistle, hum, or sing to themselves in more or less unobtrusive ways.

---

15. To have a choice of aural diversions is a matter of some importance. As the Italian sociologist Silvia Zambrini (2009) observes, people have no say in the music piped into public spaces, such as elevators, retail shops, transit depots, and so on. The sources of aural programming to which I refer here differ in that the individual has some say in the programming.

A special note is in order for a recondite solitary diversion that arguably is the most ubiquitous of them all. I refer of course to the mental peripatetics that, as I mentioned above, are forms of activity but not action. In an interview with a factory worker (also cited in note 13 of the present chapter), Studs Terkel (1972, p. 160) provides an illuminating report of how mental peripatetics help individuals to cope with the boring, solitary regimens on the shop floor. Terkel's informant explains how he copes with the din and tumult on the shop floor:

> You pretty much stay to yourself. You get involved with yourself. You dream, you think of things you've done. I drift back continuously to when I was a kid and what me and my brothers did. The things you love most are the things you drift back into. Lots of times I worked from the time I started to the time of the break and never realized I had worked.

No doubt this man speaks for most of us who have daydreamed or reminisced or let our thoughts wander where they will in order to keep ourselves occupied when performing dull, undemanding routines. Such activities may not be agentic forms of action, as indicated above, but nevertheless they are activities that enable people like Terkel's informant to cope with the boredom of highly structured yet unengaging tasks.

Diversions from regimens may serve to keep boredom at bay. But note that this begs the question of why we need diversions from boredom at all. Robert Nisbet (1982, pp. 23–24) once observed that human beings are unique in their capacity for boredom. He goes on to suggest that boredom results from a central nervous system that evolved out of the prehistoric pressure on our species to remain alert, vigilant, and aggressive. In other words, as a species we need to stay mobilized or engaged.

Whether or not Nisbet's evolutionary speculation holds up, there is solid evidence that boredom increases brain arousal (London and Schubert, 1972). Common experience supports the same point insofar as restlessness is a concomitant of boredom in many different settings. If we accept that boredom is accompanied by some measure of unmobilized neuropsychological capacity, then it is a small, logical step to suggest that diversions from undemanding regimens serve, in effect, to "soak up" this excess energy by keeping us occupied with two things at once.

We tend not to make too much of this ability to do two things at once because it is equally apparent that human beings can only fully concentrate on doing one thing at a time. But it should come as no surprise to sociologists of action that actors perform two things simultaneously when engaged in boring forms of behavior. One of Erving Goffman's cleverest insights into the individual's involvement (or it might be better to say lack of involvement) in social action turns on just this point. Goffman (1963, pp. 43–45, chaps. 3–4 passim; 1967, pp. 113–136 passim) maintained that within any situation individuals may invest the better part of their attention in what he terms a main involvement. But in uninvolving situations they may split off a small fraction of their attention for what he terms a side involvement (e.g., drawing doodles or brushing stray thread from one's clothes during a boring meeting).[16] Goffman was mainly concerned with what he idiosyncratically termed "alienation" from interaction. Nevertheless, this same bilateral capacity comes into play in coping with boring regimens as well. As Goffman would have been likely to agree, it is no easy matter to cope with the tedium of dull things.

16. A recent empirical study by British psychologist Jackie Andrade (2009) confirms Goffman's theoretical insights, albeit Goffman was more interested in the nature of action while Andrade, building on psychological research, is more interested in the workings of the mind.

But taking note of diversions from solitary regimens adds another twist. Ironically, maintaining a secondary involvement when we are by ourselves helps to steady our performance with respect to the primary involvement at hand.

DISCIPLINE

Though diversions help us cope with undemanding regimens, that is, those regimens that do not require us to invest ourselves fully in what we do, they don't help when the performance of regimens, dull and unengrossing though they may be, can be performed only when we invest ourselves fully in the task at hand. These sorts of regimens make their demands in various ways. Consider, for example, operators of heavy, cumbersome machines that require a great deal of attention and physical effort for the operator to control (e.g., pneumatic drills, floor sanders, wood chippers, and the like). Individuals who operate such machines have no choice but to be fully engaged at all times. Some regimens make fewer demands on physical strength, but more demands on flexibility and dexterity. Acquiring the basic skills necessary to play a musical instrument exemplifies such demands. To habituate herself to these skills (e.g., coordinated fingerings on strings, valves, or keys) the novice has no choice but to repetitively practice scales and simple tunes with intense concentration for long periods of time. And there are also regimens that require rapt attention but virtually no physical movement at all, such as memorizing the basic vocabulary and grammar in a new language or learning the techniques of a complex computer software program. Bear in mind that these are all regimens. There is nothing intrinsically absorbing in repeatedly playing a simple tune like "Twinkle, Twinkle, Little Star," especially when the likelihood of mistakes is high. Nor is there anything interesting about breaking pavement and chiseling holes with a pneumatic drill for eight hours a day. Thus, these regimens may be just as boring as less demanding assembly line work or driving long distance truck routes, but the problem now is not what to do with that portion of one's attention that remains unengaged. The problem is rather how to stay fully mobilized when the work is not only flat and dull but rigorous and unrelenting as well.

It is no secret that coping with boring, demanding regimens is never an easy matter. In fact, the only way to cope is through ascetic discipline, a self-imposed application to the task at hand, coupled with the suppression of impulses to procrastinate, relax, or otherwise delay or avoid the rigors of the work.[17] There is a term familiar to speakers of Yiddish and German and common enough in English usage to appear in the *Oxford English Dictionary* as well that describes the form of self-discipline and the elementary practical behavior it requires. The term is *zitzfleisch*, which the *Oxford English Dictionary* defines as the ability to endure, to persist in some capacity. The literal meaning of the term in German, which is the ability to keep one's body (flesh) seated in one place, provides a visual image of the endurance and persistence to which the term refers.

Regimens that require constant application of mental discipline are especially hard to bear. Ironically, these regimens are

17. This sense of discipline should not be confused with the expansive, ambiguous sense of discipline developed by Michel Foucault ([1975] 1977, Part 3, Ch. 1). Foucault writes of a vast set of practices that form a regime that collectively constitute a form of both domination and efficient production. As his rhetorical flourishes and exaggerations suggest, Foucault means to use the term discipline in a provocative manner. In contrast, I prefer to define discipline in a more limited and commonsensical way. Thus, whereas Foucault entertains questions about how disciplinary regimes mold and control "docile bodies," I am more interested in the ways that individuals must apply themselves to mentally or physically demanding regimens regardless of any political implications at all. For other sociological discussions of discipline see Emile Durkheim ([1925] 1973, pp. 33–79) and Max Weber ([1922] 1968, pp. 1148–1156).

most ubiquitous and unavoidable in the education of students in the primary and secondary grades. Is this a cruel form of punishment, as schoolchildren eternally have maintained? Not really. There seems to be no other way to learn foundational mathematical and verbal skills than to practice them many times through. And yet, that said, it seems that the young are confronted with more boring and tedious regimens than the more mature members of society, most of whom presumably employ the same skills without concentration at all.

The example of school drills suggests one final point that in a way expands upon my earlier proposal that regimens are mixed-motive games and therefore that we can fruitfully discuss them apart from whatever the individual's intentions or desires may be. School children who tackle repetitive mathematics drills night after night or memorize proper spelling and definitions, scientific terminology, and the chronological sequences of historical events endure these regimens for a panoply of reasons. Some are ambitious to succeed, some fear the sanctions of their parents if they fail, some want to best their siblings or friends, and some may be trying to enhance their confidence and self-esteem. Since none of these motives are mutually exclusive, it is easy to imagine many different constellations of motives among the students who complete their homework in any given class. The crux of the matter is that these motives in themselves may be necessary rather than sufficient conditions to persist with boring, dull drills. For most students, leaving out of account those with a rigidly ascetic work ethic, a moment will arrive during a boring assignment when every item must be completed in exactly the right way, when the load is heavy and long, and the powers of focused concentration on things that have no logical or narrative telos are difficult to sustain, when the student ultimately will be tempted to turn away and do something more enjoyable. Here we arrive at the disciplined solitary activity in its purest form: the ability to persist until the job is done even when the energizing force of motivation, weakened by a period of tedious work, has lost its force and begun to break down. At this point, for the student who persists and endures, staying disciplined and focused, staying seated in one place, becomes the only motive that matters.

ENGROSSMENTS

In an early section of chapter 3, we took a close look at the remarkable ability of the modest game of solitaire to capture and hold a player's attention for indefinite periods of time, win or lose, deal after deal. Solitaire, as we saw, produces nothing of any value. No problems are solved, no projects are advanced, and nothing of consequence is at stake by playing the game. People play solitaire primarily or perhaps even exclusively for its ability to absorb attention, a trait that may relieve stress, suppress anxieties, and delay the start of onerous tasks. In brief, the game occupies individuals who otherwise might find themselves at loose ends, a broad group that includes passengers waiting for (or on) planes and trains, senior citizens, hospital patients, vacationers on rainy days, and many more. To utilitarians or ascetics, solitaire may seem a waste of time, a means to dissipate energy that might be applied in more fruitful ways. But most people prefer not to live every moment of their lives on the bottom line. Most people occasionally find themselves in situations where the small comforts of a game like solitaire contribute more to their well-being than a narrow judgment, based on practicalities, might take into account.

Simple, engrossing, single-player activities are enormously popular in everyday life, though they are largely ignored by sociologists of culture. Given its presence on every computer equipped with a Windows operating system, solitaire may be the most ubiquitous single-player game in the twenty-first century world, but it is hardly the only simple form of recreation with the special ability to keep solitary individuals spellbound for shorter or longer periods of time. To the contrary, there are a surprising number of different ways to keep individuals engrossed by themselves. Consider a small survey of notable examples.

According to sources cited in the *New York Times* (Rivlin, 2004), in 2003 nearly 40 million Americans played a slot machine, almost all of them seated or standing alone before devices programmed to ensure that in the long run the machine always wins.[18] Though patrons of slot machines located in small shops and taverns may play one or two games, casinos house the vast majority of American slot machines and, as indicated below, such machines are very clearly designed to keep players occupied game after game, usually until their money runs out. Consider now an extremely different example. According to CNN, nearly 51 million Americans read romance novels each year and their purchases account for nearly 25% of annual book sales. Add to this the readers of other formulaic genres (e.g., war stories, western novels, spy thrillers, mysteries, and detective stories), and an even more sizable portion of the American reading public

18. By slot machines I use the generic reference to electronic gambling machines, including video poker machines, as well as devices in which reels are matched on each spin. More recent statistics for the number of people who play each year are not readily available. However, according to Natasha Dow Schüll (2012, p. 5) the total number of electronic gambling machines has grown from 500,000 in 1996 to 875,000 in 2008. There is, then, good reason to assume that the *New York Times* figure from 2003 underrepresents the number of people who play slot machines today.

recurrently settles down, shuts out the world, and lets an author skilled in the conventions of formulaic genre mechanically spin out a vivid, dramatic, but ultimately predictable plot.[19] Obviously, reading a formulaic novel is a quite different matter from playing solitaire or a slot machine. Nevertheless, reading these novels induces similarly absorbing effects. And the list goes on. There may be no way to determine how many people complete (or at least try to complete) various kinds of puzzles by themselves each day. But even in this age of cash-starved, shrinking newspapers, almost every daily still in print includes a crossword puzzle, and most publish numerous puzzles like Sudoku, word jumbles, and various other puzzles as well. If any additional proof is wanted for the popularity of these puzzles, one need only survey the magazine racks at supermarkets and large discount department stores. There, often prominently displayed at the checkout aisles, you will find pulp magazines filled with hundreds of the same sorts of puzzles found in the newspapers. Toy retailers carry yet more examples. Among them is the venerable jigsaw puzzle that is now 250 years old, thereby proving that engrossment in recreational activities are nothing new. And new kinds of solitary activities continue to appear. Consider simple electronic games such as *Tetris, Pac-man*, and *Space Invaders*. Once confined to large machines in commercial locales, these simple-to-play games now are available for every console and computer format, not to

19. All references to formulaic fiction exclude works with serious literary intention. For example, though Victor Hugo and Charles Dickens in the nineteenth century, and Jack London, James T. Farrell, and Tom Wolfe in the twentieth century all wrote novels that can engross readers exceptionally well, all of them deepened their engaging plots with layers of social criticism, implicit allusions to other literary and/or cultural themes, and so on. For a discussion of formulaic fiction see Mary F. Rogers (1991, p. 60 passim). Though Rogers's sociological study is meant to explore the interaction between authors and readers, and therefore she frames her discussion of formulaic fiction quite differently than the frame of solitary action I employ here, ultimately we agree on the predictable nature of formulaic works.

mention the portable game devices, complete with earphones, as well as telephone apps that have made these games a visible feature in public spaces around the world.[20]

I call the category that includes all of these activities *engrossments*, activities that offer individuals opportunities to become so fully absorbed as to be carried away. Goffman used the related term engrossables (1974, pp. 46, 57–58) to refer to activities with the ability to capture and hold the mind. However, two differences distinguish the category of engrossables to which Goffman refers from the category of engrossments to which I refer here. First, Goffman is mainly concerned with interpersonal activities such as sporting contests, chess matches, and theatrical performances rather than the solitary activities such as slot machine play, crossword puzzles, and formulaic fiction that are my primary interest. Second, and worthy of special note, whereas for Goffman engrossables captivate individuals by creating or inducing them to create small, often quite complicated phenomenological worlds, in my usage, engrossments are simple activities that, as will be evident momentarily, hold the subject's attention in more elementary ways. Thus, while opponents might say that they get lost in contemplating their strategic or tactical options during a chess match, there is only a very limited range of strategies or tactics involved in playing slot machines or completing a crossword puzzle. Then too, while a theatrical performance may challenge actors, directors, and audiences alike to ponder the ambivalence of characters, the implications in the plot, or the expressive nuances in the delivery of lines, formulaic fiction is too

20. It should be noted, that while the world of electronic games includes titles that make great demands on the individual's skills, intellect, and imagination, only the simplest games are at issue here. Thus, games of strategy such as *Halo, Doom*, and the many different simulations of sporting contests in which the player makes decisions, as would a coach, are not under consideration in these remarks.

familiar and predictable to make these observations of subtlety worthwhile. The simplicity of engrossments is a relative thing of course. To novices, the *New York Times* crossword puzzle may be a bewildering affair, but some highly experienced devotees can complete a puzzle very quickly (and in ink!). Likewise, to a beginner, completing a one–hundred-piece jigsaw puzzle may take all day, but many individuals can manage puzzles with five hundred pieces or more in a short afternoon.

The fundamental question about engrossments is: What makes them so engrossing? What is the commonly shared trait that gives such a diversity of simple recreations the ability to capture, focus, and hold the undistracted attention of so many millions of people? Figure 4.1 supplies the beginning of an answer by indicating that engrossments are tightly structured activities. But this cannot be the only dimension of the answer. After all, regimens are also tightly structured, but a distinctive feature of regimens is that they are the most dull and boring of all solitary forms of behavior. So what is the difference between the two? Recall that what makes regimens so boring is that they produce no context as they are performed. In the case of engrossments, the converse is true. That is, though every move or practice in an engrossment may be very tightly structured by rules, scripts, or other means, and though their results are preordained, engrossments leave some margin of uncertainty in every move. To put it another way, while the destiny may be fixed, no single development reveals how the final outcome will be reached. Thus, move-by-move, the activity leads the player to consider what has happened already and what will come next. In this way, this odd teleology of fixed procedures, determined outcomes, and contingent moves creates a peculiar kind of context formation. This is hardly the kind of context formation that Garfinkel discovered in his studies of conversation. In conversation every move is truly contingent, which is why conversations can move peripatetically in the manner indicated earlier in this chapter. However, the tight structuration of engrossments precludes real contingency. Conversations may go their own way, but engrossments have a destiny. In the context formation of an engrossment, individuals simply participate in the creation of their own fate (or in the case of formulaic fiction, the fate of the protagonist).

Of course every engrossment does this in its own way. Consider the jigsaw puzzle. There certainly is no doubt about the outcome: the final picture to be constructed is printed right on the box. But until the puzzle is nearly complete, every move presents a tightly structured challenge. As the puzzle proceeds, spaces are created that call for a piece of a certain size, shape, and fragment of an image. Only one piece will fill the spot. So the individual is invited to look for this piece (although, as often happens, she may serendipitously find other pieces that fill other spots along the way). Having found the right piece, she now has a new space to be filled, and the search begins again. Each piece of the puzzle changes the context that defines the need for another piece. Thus, the context keeps changing until the puzzle is complete. Formulaic fiction works in a somewhat different way. Within a chapter or two after the story begins, the novel sets a goal for the protagonist(s), such as lasting love, identifying the villain, defeating the enemy. However, obstacles and complications stand in the way. Soon the protagonists find their way into daunting and often seemingly impossible situations, and then, by fortune and fortitude, they find a way to proceed. Soon the cycle of complications and resolutions begin again and every predicament from which they escape and every challenge they meet brings them closer to the denouement. This pulp fiction form of context formation carries the reader along, wondering what will happen next and how the happy ending will arrive. Like a jigsaw puzzle, each piece of the plot brings moments of uncertainty, while the completed structure of the narrative is never in doubt.

Each engrossment has its own techniques of context formation, that is, its own way of moving forward, its own limited contingencies, and its own ultimate goal. But recent technological advances in the engineering of slot machines provide a detailed glimpse into how engrossments hold the subject's attention. Superficially, it might seem that slot machines should be able to hold their patrons simply because as a form of gambling they offer a chance to come away with more money than they began. But if gamblers made decisions based on the odds, no one would ever gamble at all. Still, there are different ways to gamble and some of them create very little context in which to become engrossed. Consider lotteries, for example. Individuals purchase their tickets and then check them against the winning numbers after the scheduled drawing is held. Though tickets can be checked in various ways, none of them take more than a few minutes. However, slot machines, and especially the high-tech casino machines, hold players much longer, often keeping them until they have lost all of the money they allotted for gaming on a given day.

How do slot machines do it?[21] To begin, slots have come a long way from the so-called "one-armed bandits" with mechanical parts and a hand-pulled lever (which may have limited long-term play to those with strong right arms). In fact, even the actual

21. For information on electronic gambling machines (slot machines in generic terms), I rely on the detailed research and subtle analysis of the play, design, and electronic software in such machines that is provided by Natasha Dow Schüll (2012, see especially Chs. 3–6). Though I had already written accounts of slot machine play in early drafts of this chapter I am pleased to acknowledge that Schüll anticipates a number of insights presented here, including her analyses of the ways in which slot machines create an experience that combines a sense of contingency and control (see below.) Indeed, Schüll's findings implicitly support the concept of engrossments I discuss here as a form of solitary action.

coin slots have disappeared from most of today's casino machines. Most machines now permit or require generic or proprietary credit cards. Having established a line of credit, the player begins what amounts to an electronically structured process of context formation that is teleologically destined to exhaust the player's available funds, provided the machine can keep the player engrossed until that goal is reached. Machines use several techniques to create an engrossing context. For one thing, the machine must sustain the illusion that any given game (i.e., spin of the reels in simple machines, deal of the cards in somewhat more complex video poker machines) may pay off with a winning combination. The majority of machines maintain this illusion by randomly producing winning games, albeit the random numbers generators used to program these outcomes are programmed to pay off at intervals and in increments that ensure a gradual loss of funds. But from one game to the next, the machine encourages an illusion of contingency. If a machine fails to pay off on any given game, the player is encouraged to believe that it may pay off on the next. And sure enough, at some point a winning game turns up. The player is thus encouraged to create momentary narratives such as the expectation that a machine that has not produced a winner for a while is "due" for a payoff. In reality, of course, random numbers generators produce only individual events, so this narrative of expectations has no basis in fact. But nonetheless, the narrative itself, supported by the occasional payoff, can keep players chasing winners for quite a long period of time.

But context formation is not limited to the expectation of a winner. If that were so, then a machine might simply flash outcomes on a screen as fast as the player could read them until a winner popped up. In this way, a player's bankroll might be exhausted in a matter of minutes, even after the occasional winning payoff is taken into account. Like solitaire players who enjoy turning the cards, or folks who like to search for their own jigsaw pieces when they know how the picture they will create will appear from the start, slot machine players become more involved in the action if they can do something that appears to produce an outcome. Two different types of slot machines do this in two different ways. Slot machines with reels provide players with buttons that stop each reel (item in a line of spinning symbols) individually. Hence, though the outcome is electronically generated (and the game is thus structured) independent of the player's moves, just as the correct match of solitaire cards is preordained by the initial shuffle of the cards, the player feels involved as a participant in the outcome even though no skill whatsoever is involved. There is actually a bit of skill in the video poker variant of slot machines. Here a player is permitted to discard and draw cards after the initial deal. An unskilled novice may lose money on every hand, but an experienced player may recurrently score small payoffs. Though these payoffs will never exceed the player's losses in the long run, they allow the experienced players to invest some skill in each move. Like crossword devotees who feel involved in a process and outcome they did not create by virtue of their skill, the video poker players are permitted to feel a sense of their own abilities as long as they stay involved in the game.

Involvement in the chase for a win is abetted by cleverly designed cues that add feedback to the process of context formation that the machines want to promote. Visual cues are, of course, built into the game. A button is pushed, and a reel is stopped or a card is turned. Then a second reel is stopped or card is turned on, and on a contingent basis a possible winner may still be in play. Thus, not only does the chase for a winner keep the player involved, but the very play of the game from one move to the next within the game advances a context much in the same way as making a match during solitaire or finding the right jigsaw piece. Indeed, I would argue that if monetary losses were not an impediment, players might stay involved in these small move-by-move episodes for hours on end as a pastime in itself. But slot machines do not rely on visual cues alone. Audio cues are added literally at every turn. One sound is triggered when a button is pushed. When possible winners turn up on the screen a more urgent sound is heard. Winners may trigger a little tune and/or more elaborate set of sounds including the prerecorded and technically enhanced sound of coins clinking in a receptacle that, of course, is not really there. By such means the video and audio cues in the play of a slot machine game provide perceptual elements to context formation that is rivaled among engrossments only by single-player video games that have a great deal in common with their slot machine cousins.

As mentioned in note 21, I am indebted to the scholarship of the anthropologist Natasha Dow Schüll in *Addiction by Design* (2012) for my account of the engrossing qualities of slot machines here. But Schüll's overarching theme shows us the dark side of slot machines that cannot be ignored. As Schüll's title suggests, the problem is addiction. Addiction here not only entails the profound consequences of financial ruin and bankruptcy, but also the physiological effects of sitting before a screen rapidly pushing buttons for hour after hour and in extreme cases even entire days at a time. Like all addictions, slot machines offer an escape from personal and emotional problems. This is not the proper place to comment on these problems at length. But as Schüll makes abundantly clear, they are often literally tragic. To conclude on slot machines, it therefore must be said that they are a unique form of engrossment. They so exploit the sense of context formation in order to extract profit that the escape they offer is one from which some people never return. Of course, engrossments are not unique in their capacity to lead to solitary compulsion. For example, some people compulsively wash their hands many times each day or compulsively seek the lowest price for an item even when they add hours to every shopping trip in order to achieve inconsequential savings. Nonetheless, there is no denying the danger of compulsion that can arise not only from slot machines but from other engrossments as well. People can spend more time than they should or can afford reading formulaic fiction, solving puzzles, or playing all manner of free solitary games. There may be no need for Sudoku forms or romance novels to come with warning labels like tobacco products, though that might not be a bad idea as far as slot machines go. But by virtue of their capacity to keep people involved, engrossments should be practiced in moderation.

Chapter 5

Forms of Solitary Action: Reflexives

REFLEXIVES AS A FORM OF SOLITARY ACTION

Red Smith, who for over half a century produced sports commentary of surpassing literary merit, was once asked how he wrote. He is reported to have replied:[1] "Writing is easy: all you do is sit staring at a blank sheet of paper until little drops of blood form on your forehead." Smith's remark buffers with ironic wit a familiar truth for writers. But his remark also suggests a seldom-posed question: What makes writing such a difficult thing to do? Why can't we just spin out some words that fall easily into place, as they sometimes do for experienced reporters who report the pertinent details of a press conference or a courtroom trial? Writing, after all, is a solitary activity. Though Smith's editors may have given him a strict deadline for his column, no editor came between him and whatever he put on his empty page. What made an accomplished journalist like Smith feel so uncomfortable about confronting this task?

---

1. Smith's quote has appeared in several variant forms. For others see Keys (2006, p. 257).

In a very generalized sense, Smith's imaginary drops of blood form for two sequentially related reasons. In the first place, Smith must come up with a hook, an angle, something that makes his column worth reading. This is the realm of intuition, inspiration, insight, a hunch, or what poets might call a word from the muse. Though few people claim any certainty about how it forms,[2] one thing is clear: the process is not conscious, it is not really under the individual's control, and hence it would be incorrect to say that any agency is involved. Consider some examples: it may occur to Smith, while watching the performance of a great prize fighter like Muhammad Ali, that it would be worth writing a column about how Ali demonstrates why boxing used to be called the "sweet science"; it might occur to Smith, as it actually did to the sports columnist Grantland Rice (1924), to compare the conquering members of a football backfield to the fearsome "Four Horseman of the Apocalypse" from the biblical book of revelations; or having been bored by a golf tournament, Smith might be moved to write about why golf is not really a sport. Whatever idea he comes up with, there is no accounting for it. It may be frightening to face a page without any idea, but writers have no choice but to rely on their intuition.

But even with an idea for a column, the page remains empty. As opposed to an epiphany, a phenomenon to which I shall return toward the end of this chapter, an intuition is vague and undeveloped by itself. So Ali demonstrates why they call boxing the "sweet science": What does that mean? So the backfield of a

2. Cognitive psychologists have opened a potentially promising way to understand the origins of intuition via a theory of the unconscious included in dual-process theory. Though studies have turned up intriguing evidence in this regard, we remain far from a full-fledged theory of how ideas originate unconsciously and surface in the conscious mind. Any survey of the psychological foundations of dual-process theory must include Kahneman (2011.) Other surveys of dual-process theories include Evans (2008) and Wilson (2002). Sociologists too have been intrigued by dual-process accounts: Vaisey (2009, 1682–1687) and DiMaggio (1997).

football team resembles the "Four Horseman of the Apocalypse": How so? And indignant golfers everywhere want to know: Just why doesn't golf qualify as a sport? Now the hard work of filling the page actually begins. The sportswriter must come up with reasons, unpack a metaphor, compose an argument. Moreover, the entire column must be more than a potpourri of random thoughts. The development must be structured, organized so that subsidiary insights emerge and the overall point is satisfyingly made. This sort of action is more agentic, more under the author's control. If the columnist carries the development in one direction and this doesn't pan out, then the thing to do is to go back and try another line. On this count, a writer is a spinner of webs with words. And like the spider, a writer must work hard to spin a web that serves its purpose, in this case to fill the page with a column that's worthwhile.[3]

Composing sports columns so that they develop an intuition into a coherent, satisfying piece of work is an example of the fourth form of solitary action featured in Figure 4.1 in chapter 4. For reasons I explain in the next section, I call activities that fall within this form "reflexives." A glance back at Figure 4.1 will show that the category of reflexives is characterized by what may seem at first to be an unlikely pair of traits: high involvement and loose structuration. That is to say, a high degree of involvement in a quite unstructured process of context formation. Sportswriting, on Smith's account, exhibits each of these qualities in an easily grasped way. On the one hand, the empty page, lacking any substance of its own, sits in front of Smith waiting,

3. In a widely quoted apothegm regarding the relation of inspiration to the work of developing an idea into a finished form, Thomas Edison once remarked: "Genius is one percent inspiration, ninety-nine percent perspiration." Mr. Edison may be guilty of some exaggeration here. But, his sense that inspiration is insufficient in itself to produce or create much of anything at all is surely correct.

or in a sense even asking, to be filled. On the other hand, Smith sits before the empty page in intense concentration, an intense concentration that this kind of project virtually demands if it is to be accomplished at all.

Smith's tongue-in-cheek dramatic imagery of beads of blood should not blind us to the prevalence of reflexives in many quarters of modern life. In the household we find solitary individuals troubleshooting balky appliances that mysteriously refuse to work, and others who create original recipes from scratch. On construction sites we find plumbers, electricians, and tradespeople who improvise means to complete their job assignments when unforeseen obstacles make routine solutions impossible. In the office, executives create novel business plans, lawyers compose clever briefs, and administrators sometimes reorganize their departments. Engineers, computer programmers, architects, and so on are valued for their proficiency at solving problems and producing orderly, workable, and functional outcomes on projects where glitches, bugs, and steady streams of unforeseen complications threaten to bring work to a halt. Finally, we have reflexives in their purest form: projects undertaken in the arts, sciences, and humanities. Here we find analogs to Smith's blank page in an especially pure form. Consider the experimental scientist who must devise a novel means to test an unorthodox hypothesis, the poet trying to find ways to develop in her head the vague but compelling trope or metaphor, the critic who is stirred and excited by a new film but finds it difficult to say just why the production worked so well for him or her.

Reflexives like these differ markedly from their three counterparts in the forms of solitary action in Figure 4.1. Unlike regimens and engrossments, they provide no preformatted structure to carry the individual along. An individual playing solitaire, for example, never has to worry about what to do next: the steps in the game are all defined in advance. But what to do next is precisely the question an individual must answer when confronted by an uncooperative washing machine. Unlike peripatetics and more undemanding regimens, to engage in reflexives, the individual's powers of concentration must be fully absorbed. An executive composing a business model must keep in mind that part of the plan that she has already completed if she is to successfully put the rest of the plan together. This demand for intense concentration is what makes reflexives such hard work. Indeed, there is no need for a cognitive psychology study to know that we have limits to our powers of concentration. As Hannah Arendt (1977, p. 4) once wrote, anyone attempting to continuously live the life of the mind would soon find herself exhausted.

REFLEXIVE LINES OF THOUGHT

Most people would agree that writing, troubleshooting, creating recipes, designing bridges, and so on are forms of action. But it is more difficult to say what these actions share in common when they are performed. The short-form answer is that performing these actions involves a distinctive kind of contextual reflexivity, a kind of contextual reflexivity well suited to the activities of individuals on their own. But since this kind of contextual reflexivity has seldom been discussed, it will be useful to introduce it in a measured way rather than simply to provide a concise, technical definition here.

To begin, though in many cases reflexives result in material outcomes and require material maneuvers of various kinds, such as improvising a solution to a plumbing problem, designing a new piece of computer hardware, or planning the effective use of space in a warehouse, these reflexives and all others require mental work. We can envision this mental work in terms of commonly used figures of speech such as lines of thought, trains of thought, streams of thought, and so on. The salient point about these figures of speech is that they all suggest some sort of development sequence, an ongoing development that occurs at least in some leading respects in the mind. Of course, like most figures of speech, we must avoid taking notions of streams or flows or trains of thought too literally. For example, lines of thought need not be developed in a linear manner. As will be evident in examples to come, lines of thought in reflexive projects may shift directions, double back upon themselves, or even tentatively test developments on themes along several different paths. Then too, images of trains and streams suggest processes of development that remain in constant motion like a river or a string of railway cars. But this too is misleading, a point underscored by William James, who is well-known for his references to "streams of consciousness." Shortly after introducing the phrase in *Principles of Psychology* ([1890] 1981, p. 236), James revises and re-specifies the kind of motion of thought he has in mind, conceiving the motion as more like how we see the lives of birds, alternating between dynamic flight and perching at rest. To cite a prosaic example: people employed in white-collar jobs may concentrate on a cognitive task at work (e.g., working out a design, diagnosing a problem with a machine, composing an administrative plan); leave the task incomplete at the end of the workday; go home, relax, and then pursue a different line of thought; then return the next morning and pick up the threads of the original task at hand. Finally, it bears repeating that lines of thought originate with intuitions or insights. But the latter are generally vague and undeveloped. We produce lines of thought in the process of developing something substantial from the evanescent notion from which it began. This difference is also evident in that one need not concentrate to have good ideas. As Max Weber once observed ([1918] 1946, p. 136): "ideas come when they please, not when it pleases us." Weber goes on to point out that ideas frequently occur to us as we relax (e.g., on a sofa or when taking a walk). This could hardly be more different than producing a line of thought. For this, to repeat, we need intense and sustained concentration. It is hard to imagine an architect designing a segment of a substantial building while taking a walk, or a computer programmer writing a program from front to back while lying on a sofa.

Developing lines of thought requires sustained, focused, concentrated effort. But effort alone is not enough. Any given kind of project or task requires the application of a set of culturally specific skills, some purely mental and others implicating lines of thought in material practices. Cognition and material activity combine in many different projects from fine arts, like painting and sculpture, to more modest craftwork, such as creating a custom cake design for a wedding or birthday. Jazz improvisations on piano or other instruments involve mind and body as well. But in other projects material practices recede. It is fair to say that, though some sort of writing instrument is involved, most of the action in composing literary works goes on in the mind. The same goes for marketing strategies; investment plans; legal arguments; making domestic plans for vacations or family celebrations; and projecting household spending against expected income. But whether they are purely mental or combine mind and body, notice the specific skills that each of these tasks involves. Knowing how to write a novel has little in common with developing a legal argument or creating a wedding cake. More broadly, the skills involved in most activities are indigenous to modern culture, or more often, specific subgroups in which members learn to develop certain kinds of thought in specialized ways.

At this point we see that reflexive tasks and projects involve the culturally skillful development of thought. The question now is: How does this development occur? And here we arrive at the notion of contextual reflexivity from which reflexives as a form of solitary action take their name. Contextual reflexivity is not unique to solitary action. The phenomenon was initially discovered and documented in Harold Garfinkel's original studies in ethnomethodology, many of which concerned the turn-by-turn or move-by-move production of context in conversation. Garfinkel (1963; 1967) demonstrated that conversations are reflexively structured as each turn of talk proceeds. That is to say, each interjection makes sense only within the local context created by previous interjections. But this context is only loosely structured. There is no one thing that must be said next. A conversationalist needs to exercise some degree of improvisation here. What is true for conversations is true for the reflexive form of solitary action as well. Consider the instance of jazz musicians as discussed in chapter 3. A jazz theme may begin with a refrain from a certain melody, but the jazz musician has at hand a variety of options for pursuing variations that may more or less radically alter the original melodic context, riff by riff or phrase by phrase, as the line of music unfolds. The same holds true for Red Smith writing a sports column. Having decided, let us say, to write a column on how Muhammad Ali epitomizes the "sweet science" of boxing, Smith might begin with a paragraph on how boxing as a "sweet science" should be understood and close the paragraph by observing that he has never seen a finer example of the "sweet science" of boxing than he did last night when Muhammad Ali fought in Madison Square Garden. In a single paragraph Smith has created a good bit of context, tying grand thoughts about the art of boxing to a specifically situated match. The context is reflexive:

in one sense Smith is committed to writing about how Ali's performance last night epitomizes what boxing should be about. But on the other hand, he has created possibilities to say many different things in his next paragraph. For example, he might say that Ali moved with an efficiency that conserved his energy while his opponent tired himself out. Then again, he might notice that Ali is one of the few boxers to understand that footwork combining strategy, speed, and grace is more valuable to a boxer than a stunning knockout punch. Or he might shift elliptically from one point to the next. The column has more context now, but there are new possibilities as well. Smith might move to a transcendent performance by Ali in a particular round that approached platonic boxing perfection and then create an opening for further development by observing that, even as Ali moves with efficiency, grace, and speed, he seems thoughtful, as if he were devising new tactics and strategy while he exchanged blows with his opponent in the center of the ring. Smith then proceeds to a riff on how most fans underestimate the cerebral side of boxing, and so it goes until the column is complete and the page is filled.

As the example suggests, reflexive contextuality in the reflexive form of solitary action both resembles yet differs from reflexive contextuality in conversation. Like conversation, at any given moment the actor must take account of whatever has come before and integrate each move so that it makes sense in terms of that previous context. This is as true for a computer programmer or a jazz improviser or an engineer designing a bridge as it is for a writer. Again, like a conversationalist, there is no single necessary way to proceed to the next move. There are many ways to proceed. But unlike contextual reflexivity in conversation, individuals are on their own; they must create the context and keep it moving all by themselves.

The solitary form of contextual reflexivity has both advantages and disadvantages, compared with conversation. On the positive side, the individual is free to develop independent lines of thought. In a conversation, any given participant is to some extent at the mercy of whatever new topics other participants introduce to move the conversation along. I may mention something about how gracefully Muhammad Ali danced around the ring, and someone else might mention something about the elegance of a particular dancer at the performance of a ballet. When my next turn at talk arrives, the context may have shifted several times so that there is no longer any viable opportunity to talk again about the grace of Muhammad Ali. The difference is similar to all kinds of work that may be done by a solitary individual on the one hand or by a committee on the other. A committee where collegial rules give each participant an equal voice will seldom follow the line of thought of a single individual. Solitary action allows the individual to build a consistent context as he or she goes along. The advantage is not so much that of expressive individuality. After all, some people may develop a line of thought on a given subject better than others. The advantage instead lies in continuity. A single individual can sustain a coherent line of thought better than a group.

The disadvantage, of course, is the converse of the advantage: the individual pursuing a line of thought has only herself on whom to rely. There is certainly no reason to believe that pursuing a line of contextual development by oneself ensures a satisfactory result. For every great invention that succeeds, there must be hundreds that fail. Even great columnists like Smith must have columns they wish had never seen the light of day. Then too, the solitary individual runs the risk of creating a context that winds up as a dead end. This seldom happens in interpersonal conversations. If the conversation turns dull or verges on topics that might hurt or offend, there are many tactful strategies to change the subject before the conversation gets into trouble or breaks down. Solitary actors have means to avoid trouble as well. But since there is no one else to stave off threats of trouble before they become realities, the solitary individual is solely responsible for avoiding problems in context development or providing remedies for them when they occur. There will be more to say on problems and predicaments in context formation later on in the chapter.

It may be worthwhile to mention one more correspondence between conversation and solitary context formation, but this time with a philosophical twist. As Harold Garfinkel (1967, Ch. 8) made clear, there is nothing necessarily rational, at least in the scientific or formal logical sense of the term, about everyday activities. Conversations, as we have just noted, may jump from one topic to another (e.g., from boxing to ballet) with nothing more than an elective affinity to effect the transition from one subject to the next. The same can be true in the process of solitary context formation, which is to say that lines of thought may build context in many different ways. Does this mean that rationality never enters into solitary reflexive context formation? It depends on the nature of the activity. Formal logic, scientific reasoning, or utilitarian cost-benefit analysis rarely play any prominent role in the production of a jazz improvisation, the creation of a novel recipe, or the design for a wedding cake. However, for the mathematician trying to solve a difficult problem or a capitalist entrepreneur composing a business plan, tight logical reasoning may be an invaluable means to develop a successful line of thought from one contextual move to the next. Turning to another philosophy of action, what can we say about pragmatic steps of learning as the most suitable way to form context by trial and error? Again, it depends. Trial and error may be the only way to winnow down the possible reasons why a mysteriously inoperative washing machine refuses to run. By the same token, trial and error may be the best means to figure out which ingredient is making the new soup turn sour when it should be sweet. But pragmatic steps may not be as helpful if we are trying to build an expressive context of some kind. Recall that one of the basic things an aspiring jazz improviser must learn is what sort of musical melodies, phrases, transitions, and so on "sound like" jazz. These implicit conventions are neither rational nor pragmatic; they provide a means, or perhaps a better term is a sensibility, to guide aesthetic expression. No doubt those who create custom designs for wedding cakes have their own expressive sensibility that enables them to move step by step toward original and impressive designs, while avoiding design elements that might spell wedding cake disaster. In the end, there is no reason why an extended sequence of reflexive context formation should rely on any one philosophical principle of action at all. As we build contexts one move at a time, we are free to be philosophically promiscuous. For example, mathematicians often report that they strive for a kind of aesthetic "elegance" in their reasoning, while wedding cake designers, who certainly do strive for a very different kind of elegance, may need a few rounds of pragmatic trial and error to determine that the ornate pediments they have designed to rise from each tier will support the weight of the subsequent tiers that ascend to the top.

THE LOOSE STRUCTURATION OF SOLITARY REFLEXIVES

Loose structuration is a defining characteristic of reflexive projects. By loose structuration I mean that for some stretch of contextual development the individual is required to improvise, to create order of some kind where there is no fixed and obvious way for the context to unfold in one way rather than another. Consider in this regard reflections taken from an interview with the Pulitzer Prize–winning author Richard Russo[4] on how he begins a novel:

> Most of my novels begin with characters in some sort of dramatic situation that I don't know how to resolve . . . [later]. . . . And so you just kind of have faith. You give them life, you set them loose in the world, and you have to trust as much as you can that they will come back to you with the answer that you don't possess. . . . I try to write the way I read, in order to find out what happens next. What these people are to each other, and what they are to the story. And structure is one of the things that I always hope will reveal itself to me.

For Russo, and presumably for many other novelists as well, a novel begins with virtually no structural development in view. Notice how little this initial inspiration gives him to go on. He neither knows how to resolve his characters' predicaments nor how his characters relate to each other; nor does he have an overall narrative organization in mind to provide continuity for the stories he has yet to tell.[5] Like the jazz musician who has played nothing more than an opening melody, the work ahead must be improvised. In effect, Russo is creating a structure with a set of orderly narratives that will have orderly forms that may not be fully shaped until the process of composing the novel has

4. Richard Russo was awarded the Pulitzer Prize in 2002 for his novel *Empire Falls*. He has written many other novels as well, including *Nobody's Fool*, which in 1994 was produced as a motion picture starring Paul Newman, Melanie Griffith, and Bruce Willis.

5. Most of Russo's novels develop a number of interwoven story lines.

come to an end. Thus, part of Russo's art is building a set of realistically organized events where no order or organization had existed before.

The contextual reflexivity in this process is both an asset and a burden. Though Russo claims that he proceeds like a reader, wondering what will happen next, this way of envisioning the writing process overlooks some crucial parts of the task. At any given point in his storytelling Russo must bear in mind all sorts of elements he has already established in the novel. After all, his characters have certain personality traits and specific kinds of relationships, and certain meaningful events have happened that have had some consequence for the way in which future events unfold. Russo may believe that structure "reveals" itself to him. But in reality, he cannot build elements in the structure of the novel without maintaining continuity, and hence, some sort of organized relation with the elements he has already put in place. But these elements do not simply weigh down the storytelling with demands that they be taken into account. They are also assets to developing narrative structure. For example, once characters have certain trajectories in their development, questions arise about what might happen should their trajectories converge, or as the case may be, collide. Many novelists, and certainly Russo among them, opt to tell stories in which there is only a moderate amount of dramatic tension, in which it sometimes seems that one thing happens after another. But there is more structural order here than this phrase suggests. Not just anything can happen after other episodes have transpired. Even the shaggiest of shaggy dog stories ends up having an order or organization of some kind.

This example, like other examples drawn from the way people work in the arts, sciences, and humanities, is quite useful because a distinctive feature of such fields is that individuals have the luxury of being free to develop an inspiration into any sort of full-fledged composition in any way they like. This is not to say that such projects necessarily succeed. Most artists and scholars have given up the ghost after repeated attempts to make something out of what initially seemed like a promising idea. Moreover, the more one develops an intellectual work in an original way, the more vulnerable one becomes to conventional lines of criticism. There is security in developing contexts using standard methods and techniques, as is true for example in what Thomas Kuhn (1970) termed "normal science" or what art critics sometimes label as "derivative work." Nonetheless, every artist or thinker at least has the right, should she or he choose, to move in an original direction and develop something new.

But while examples from the arts, sciences, and humanities offer the purest—and hence the most instructive—examples of reflexive projects pursued by solitary actors, it is misleading to think that one must have their degree of unfettered freedom in order to engage in reflexive work at all. Many projects and tasks that are in some respects subject to externally imposed constraints leave open loosely structured segments that a given individual is expected to fill in. For example, an architect may be commissioned to design a house for a particular plot of land, to not exceed a certain price, and to serve various functional purposes that the client requests. But these inflexible constraints still leave many options open to design the house in one way or another. The constraints, of course, must not be forgotten as the architect moves forward one step to the next in composing the design. But part of the art in architecture is precisely the ability to realize an aesthetic vision within whatever limits a client may impose. What is true for architects is true for many other fields in engineering and other applied sciences, technical arts, marketing, advertising, and others. The high school teacher who devises a new way to present a prescribed curriculum to a class is engaged in a reflexive project. So too is the epidemiologist assigned to find the cause of the outbreak of a disease that no one has ever seen before. Where should she begin? Which variables shared by the diseased victims may lead back to its origin? Unlike a novelist who is free to write about any disease she or he likes, real or imagined, the epidemiologist must work with a fixed set of symptoms exhibited by a certain set of patients. Moreover, the epidemiologist in many respects must create a context that moves in the opposite direction from a novel. Whereas a novelist like Russo starts with some characters in a dramatic situation and then works out how the circumstances of their lives unfold, an epidemiologist begins at the end, that is, the point where a set of people have a disease, and proceeds backward in their lives to determine where the disease began.

THE PLEASURES AND PROBLEMS
OF CONTINUOUS STRUCTURATION

Producing continuity and order from beginning to end in a complicated project is seldom easy. True, everyone can name a handful of exceptional individuals whose prodigious collections of stellar works suggests that many pieces must have been produced from start to finish with little trouble at all. Shakespeare, Mozart, and Picasso impress us as much with their ability to produce multi-layered wonderful works in very brief periods of time as by the exceptional qualities of any single piece. But the world would be populated with many more successful plays, symphonies, paintings, and so on if the majority of artists and thinkers possessed these very rare talents. Even works of transcendent genius, such as symphonies by Beethoven and Brahms or Darwin's *Origins of the Species*, required extended periods of working and reworking that demonstrate just how demanding reflexive, solitary activity can be. It seems fair to say that far more often than not, the development of finished works from loosely structured origins proceeds more in fits and starts than by continuous structuration.

Yet, sequences of continuous structuration—smoothly produced lines of development where context and action advance in a steady, well-integrated stream—should not be set aside as exclusively the rare gift of the extraordinary individual. For one thing, continuous productivity is the reflexive ideal. For each actor, at least the hope if not the expectation that every move in an unfolding sequence will fit right in to the immediate sequence, and that each sequence will complement and add something of value to the work as a whole, is a necessary supposition of reflexive work. After all, if a step, a sequence, or even an entire line of development seems futile, this means that the individual has no strategy to pursue, or at best a strategy in which she or he fails to see much potential.[6] But continuous structuration is more than an ideal. In fact, while it may take unique gifts to complete an entire project in a continuous process uninterrupted by doubts, dilemmas, and dead ends, more limited episodes of continuous structuration may be encountered during the course of many different kinds of reflexive production. David Sudnow, whose insights into his own training as a player of improvisational jazz provided food for thought in chapter 3, recollects an

---

6. Hope matters a great deal in many other forms of social action as well. For a thoughtful and highly original essay on this theme, see Mische (2009).

occasion (1981, p. 85) well along in the refinement of his skills when he found himself spinning out a jazz riff in a continuously flowing way:

> For a brief course of time while playing rapidly along, a line of melody would be generated . . . a line of melody whose melodicality was not, at least it seemed, being expressly done as in my reiterative attempts to sustain continuities. An ordering of notes, stating a succession of chords, being melodic [in the language of jazz].

This brief episode of melodic improvisation clearly caught Sudnow by surprise. Quick, creative, and spontaneous, the occasion might easily be mistaken for a momentary intuition. But that is not quite what's going on. Intuitions arrive, often instantaneously, as a more or less vague sense that some item (a character in a novel, a scientific hypothesis, a legal strategy) has promising possibilities. An intuition may inspire development during a project, but it has to be unpacked and elaborated, its implications must be spelled out, and its possibilities and constraints must be probed and explored if the intuition is to be developed and incorporated into an orderly work. Sudnow's patch of spontaneous melody-making unfolded in time in a fully coherent sequence. There was nothing of the vague intuition about it; the notes were ordered and organized as a snatch of melody, fell into place note by note, albeit they fell into place at a rapidly flowing pace.

What is going on here is a kind of reflexive music-making in a loosely structured situation. How is it reflexive? It is reflexive in the sense that Sudnow played this snatch of melody in the midst of an ongoing musical context, a line of melody he had been playing along rapidly. In jazz, a melody is like a topic of conversation: at any point in the conversation certain ways of adding to the theme make sense, others sound wrong, and some don't follow at all. Conversationalists are not born knowing what sounds right or wrong. But with enough practice any competent individual learns not only what sounds right or wrong, but also how to spin out a sequence of contextually consistent phrases and even full lines of thought, and occasionally contextually appropriate stories complete with narrative structures and embedded themes. As a solo piano player, Sudnow, of course, was not conversing with anyone else. However, his training as a jazz musician had reached the point where he could spontaneously interject his own melodic sequence into the development of the music as he played along. Like a skilled conversationalist, Sudnow's jazz training had taught him suitable sets of phrases, some conventional, others idiomatic, that he was able to fit together well in certain contexts. Similarly skillful yet tacit abilities are what enable individuals in many different fields to engage in solitary episodes of continuous reflexive activity.

When Sudnow played his melodic improvisation, it was fully integrated into the ongoing line of music that came before and after his spontaneous stretch of continuous structuration. But episodes of continuous structuration do not necessarily fit smoothly into a context. In some cases an individual may be able to continuously spin out one thread of a multi-stranded context, but may then need to pause to consider how (or if) the spontaneously spun thread meshes with other contextual elements that this line of continuous structuration left out of account. My abstract description of these complications comes to life in Richard Russo's discussion of how he writes scenes in his novels.

> What comes for me is dialogue. Sometimes when my characters are speaking to me, I have to slow them down so that I'm not simply taking dictation. I have to constantly remind

myself to see the story as clearly as I hear it. The physical world in which these characters live is as important as what they're saying and doing. When I let my characters talk too fast, I make the kinds of mistakes that end up costing me days of work.

The characters' voices Russo hears, like the melodic phrases that come to Sudnow's fingertips, are spontaneous yet reflexive. Having imagined certain characters, Russo is able to sit by himself in a room and lines of conversation between them rapidly unfold in his mind. But Russo writes the kind of novels that proceed through numerous, almost cinematic settings that often have significant implications for what is going on at that point in the novel. Moreover, characters cross back and forth between locales and interwoven plot lines and it is part of his skill as a novelist that Russo makes sure that readers always know where they are and what is going on. Russo apparently has the ability to produce dialogue among his characters in a continuously flowing manner. But to develop richly textured contexts, he knows that he must modulate and control his talent for hearing his characters speak. This would be less of a problem if Russo were composing a film script (which he sometimes does). Filmmaking involves a division of labor in which other people are responsible for the visual elements of the context and sometimes even the sequencing of scenes in the plot. But a novelist is responsible for all contextual elements, and it is more difficult to unfold full-fledged situations and episodes in a continuous stream than to take dictation from the voices in one's head. The same thing is true more generally of reflexive projects of many different kinds. An individual may have a stream of coherent development for a while. But at some point one must look back over one's shoulder to see what may have been overlooked or underdeveloped.

Russo's awareness of the errors and omissions that may follow when the individual is carried away by a continuous stream of reflexive productivity suggests a cautionary note regarding Mihaly Csikszentmihalyi's well-known account of "flow" as an optimal experience in human life. Csikszentmihalyi (1990, p. 4) defines flow as "the state in which people are so involved in an activity that nothing else seems to matter, the experience itself is so enjoyable that people will do it even at a great cost for the sheer sake of doing it." Based on interviews from research subjects, Csikszentmihalyi (1990, p. 49ff) reports a variety of conditions associated with the experience of flow including: a goal-oriented activity[7] for which the individual possesses the requisite skills; the individual's freedom to concentrate on the task; and the experience of concentration as a deep, effortless involvement. Such conditions potentially apply to a multitude of activities and Csikszentmihalyi by no means wants to confine the potential for the experience of flow to the reflexive kinds of activities at issue here. Indeed, he devotes one chapter (1990, Ch. 7) to the experience of flow in work regimens and another (1990, Ch. 5) to the experience of flow through activities of the body such as athletics, dance, and sex. Though Csikszentmihalyi almost certainly would include Sudnow's experience of his first piano improvisations and Russo's experience of hearing voices dictating his fictional dialogues as fine examples of flow, he is not much concerned with processes of structuration or the qualities of the context such processes may develop. He is concerned with the virtues of the psychological experience itself. As he informs readers in the opening chapter of *Flow* (1990, pp. 16–22)—a book written with a general audience in mind—Csikszentmihalyi sees the production of flow, however it may be accomplished, as an antidote to the stressful discontents and frustrations of contemporary life.

7. According to Csikszentmihalyi (1990, p. 55) such goals need not be well defined, especially in creative work.

That flow is a joyous experience is true beyond doubt. Even the brief passages by Sudnow and Russo cited above convey the pleasure it brings. But at least as far as reflexive projects are concerned, Csikszentmihalyi may overrate the virtues of the experience. The lasting satisfaction of a reflexive project or task is the accomplishment of the activity. There may be joy in the process of writing a novel, designing a software program, or constructing a wedding cake. But the deeper satisfaction comes when the job is complete. There is an exaggerated quality to Csikszentmihalyi's belief in the virtues of flow. Even an altogether frustrating activity like devising a "workaround" for a faulty piece of plumbing or the trial-and-error process of finding a lost set of keys induces a pleasure of its own when the "workaround" succeeds or the keys are found. Moreover, as Russo suggests, getting carried away by the flow of the work may impede reflexive work, creating irritating problems and predicaments that cause the individual to work harder and longer than he or she otherwise would. This is not to pour cold water on peak experiences of flow. Not only are these moments joyful, they sometimes take the form of creative bursts that can be invaluable to moving a reflexive project along. But as we are about to see, reflexive projects can be stressful at times, and in such cases, to pursue flow for its own sake would make individuals intolerant of the intrinsic demands that come with many forms of solitary, reflexive action.

COPING WITH PREDICAMENTS: HARD WORK IN REFLEXIVE PROJECTS

Imagine you are an epidemiologist at work to design a research project to determine the cause of an outbreak of a strange, previously unknown disease with recent incidents reported in quite different locales on several different continents. Your initial analyses of the data yield ambiguous results. What do you do next? Now imagine you are a sculptor carving a valuable piece of stone only to discover half way through the project a deep internal flaw that prevents you from completing the figure as you planned. What do you do to save the project? Now imagine you are close to finishing a biography when newly discovered documents and records threaten to undermine your interpretation of pivotal episodes in your subject's life. How do you respond? Meeting the challenges posed by predicaments and problems like these constitute hard work in reflexive projects. Peripatetics and engrossments impose no analogous demands. Even regimens, as tedious as they may be, provide a well-defined set of steps required to meet the demands of the task at hand. Moreover, continuous structuration is out of the question here. To solve these problems involves creating lines of development when the road ahead is unclear, recovering from dead ends, and reconfiguring wayward developments, all of which require sustained concentration and well-organized lines of thought. Such work is marked by pauses for reflection rather than a steady flow of developments. Though it may be difficult to observe the individual as she or he confronts these problems and predicaments, nonetheless, a lot of concentrated activity is going on. This is not to say that the problems that evoke this intense concentration are always equally daunting or dire. Most projects leave blank spots within lines of reasoning, empty patches within an artistic frame, bugs in the software that must be worked out, naked assertions that must be scaled back with qualifications, and so on. These mundane problems may be trying and irritating, but they can be managed one by one, with patience and skill, like a fisherman untangling knots in a net.

One seldom reads first-person accounts of the hard work in reflexive projects. Understandably, most people would rather discuss the fine points of their completed projects than the plans that went awry, the false starts that didn't work out, the oversights they filled in, or the moments when they weren't sure what to do next or even what had gone wrong. Thomas Kuhn is a striking exception to the rule. The following passages, one in this section and one in the next, appear in a well-known essay (1977). Not only does Kuhn offer honest insights in how he met and managed the predicaments in his work; he compares how he met and managed these challenges in two different disciplines.[8] These disciplines, the history and philosophy of science, initially may seem to be closely aligned. But for Kuhn the problems he encountered in each discipline were radically distinct. Though he compares these problems in one extended passage,[9] it is more helpful to separate the two in order to make two separate points about the development of solitary, reflexive projects here. In the first excerpt Kuhn (1977, pp. 8–9) discusses how he composes historical works.

> Books, documents, and other records must be located and examined; notes must be taken, organized, and organized again. Months or years may go into work of this sort. But the end of such work is not . . . the end of the creative process. Selected and condensed notes cannot simply be strung together

8. It is a testimony to his originality and depth of his thought that a half-century after Kuhn published his most ambitious works in history (1957) and philosophy (1962, revised in 1970), they continue to shape the course of development in both fields.

9. Prior to this passage Kuhn also offers remarks on the writing of scientific reports. Since, as Kuhn (1977, p. 8) suggests, scientific writing often involves summaries of projects that are already done, I have chosen to omit them from consideration here.

to make a historical narrative. Furthermore, though chronology and narrative structure usually permit the historian to write steadily from notes and outlines for a considerable period, there are almost always key points at which his pen or typewriter refuses to function and his undertaking comes to a dead stop. Hours, days, or weeks later he discovers why he had been unable to proceed. Though his outline tells him what comes next, and though his notes provide all requisite information about it, there is no viable transition to that next part of the narrative from the point at which he has already arrived. Elements essential to the connection have been omitted from an earlier part of the story because at that point the narrative structure did not demand them. The historian must therefore go back, sometimes to documents and note taking, and rewrite substantial parts of the paper in order that the connection to what comes next may be made. Not until the last page is written can he be altogether sure that he will not have to start again, perhaps from the very beginning.

Kuhn's shadow foil in these remarks is the naïve belief that historical studies can be prepared without much intellectual effort by simply narrating a chronology in which events virtually line themselves up in a smooth, seamless order, leaving the historian little to do but to write with clarity in an engaging style and to tell the story well. But for Kuhn, writing history is a matter of assembling and sustaining historical patterns from a mass of loosely structured evidence that by no means tells its own story or organizes itself. Indeed, Kuhn suggests that the hard work of composing a historical study is there from the start. The first stage of a historical project is not simply to gather the best possible evidence, but rather to structure the evidence and to arrange the information at hand so as to develop overarching themes and smaller embedded patterns. Of course, from the start one may have some ideas about suitable themes and possible patterns. After all, an economic historian like Max Weber would not have delved so deeply into the theologies of peripheral Protestant sects without some intuitive hunch that these creeds had some bearing on substantial changes in the culture and organization of early modern economic life.[10] But the intuitive hunch is to find such patterns in the evidence or to refashion major themes when the initial hunch doesn't pan out. But for Kuhn, as almost surely for other historians, the most difficult challenges arise from the oversights, contradictions, and inconsistencies that don't become visible until the development of thematic patterns is well underway. Escaping these predicaments often involves circling back and forth to reconcile earlier and later portions of the work. It is not surprising that historians often recognize the need for additional development and support at moments of transition. Like an acrobat swinging from one trapeze to the next, the historian must make a graceful leap across empty space from one segment of the narrative to another. Acrobats, of course, meticulously plan and prepare these transitions in advance to ensure success. If something is wrong with the apparatus or the rigging, then changes must be made before the leaps begin. Historians do likewise. As Kuhn suggests, difficult transitions, for which no line of development seems clear, signal that more preparation needs to be developed in materials that came before. Moreover, any change in the balance or organization of earlier narrative lines may necessitate secondary or even tertiary revisions in other segments of the work. And since

10. Sociologists sometimes neglect the fact that Weber was trained as an economic historian, published his earliest works on the agrarian economies of ancient and medieval societies, and continued to lecture and write on economic themes throughout his career. For a biographical account of Weber's training and early economic work see Radku ([2005] 2009 Ch. 4 passim).

these problems and predicaments only come to light when they are made explicit at specific junctures in certain lines of development, the need for internal revisions may arise even in the concluding sections of an historical piece. In the terms I use here, it is an unwise historian who ever forgets the contextual reflexivity of her work, and an unsuccessful historian who is unable to meet the challenges that developing reflexive contexts entail.

Historical projects are hardly unique in the demands that various kinds of reflexive contextual development may impose. One can imagine, for example, accountants working to develop a complex report that will minimize a corporation's or wealthy client's tax burden, circling back and forth through different lines of expenditures and income, shifting funds from category to category as the law allows, in order to see which configuration works best. Indeed, one of the virtues of Excel and other accounting software programs is that they enable the consequences of changes in any given context to be observed in all other categories as well. Architects and engineers need to circle back and forth in the contextual developments when writing their plans. Here again, computer software (CAD) lightens the burden of changing, on the fly, dimensions in a plan. Nonetheless, the judgment and ingenuity of the individual remain indispensable at many junctures in the work. Computers are less helpful for other kinds of work, such as developing a strategy for litigation at a trial or composing a symphony. Here, as in the case of the historian, the contextual lines of continuity are in the hands of the individual alone and so are the solutions to the problems that inevitably arise in the reflexive development of contexts.[11]

11. Some of the examples cited in this paragraph, including accountants, architects, lawyers, and engineers, sometimes work in units or small groups and other times work by themselves. Here I refer only to projects where the work involves solitary action. It might be interesting to compare how similar contexts are developed and contextual problems and predicaments are confronted and resolved by individuals on the one hand and groups working together on the other.

Of course, as Kuhn's remarks suggest, it would be an exaggeration to say that reflexive projects simply raise challenge after challenge from step one until the project is completed. There are sequences in which the lines ahead are well defined and trouble free. For the historian the evidence is strong and complete, the narrative is straightforward, and the function of the section for the project as a whole is clear. These are episodes when, in Csikszentmihalyi's sense of the term, the work may flow. This alternation of smooth sailing and heavy seas is one reason why it is often difficult in reflexive projects to measure a good day's work in terms of the progress the individual makes. To continue with the writing of history as an example, on some days the individual may complete a number of pages in a continuous line. The individual may spend another day, or even another week or month, as Kuhn suggests, trying to figure out where an inconsistency begins or how a graceful transition can be made.

REFLEXIVE ACTION AND EPIPHANIES

We have already encountered episodes of continuous structuration during the course of reflexive projects when developments proceed so smoothly that it seems every move (e.g., brush stroke, musical phrase, line of software code, engineering solution) seems almost preordained to both follow and advance the line of thought underway. These episodes of concentrated yet free-flowing thought provide the individual with feelings of pleasure that are an intrinsically satisfying aspect of producing reflexive work. But nothing an individual ever encounters during the course of reflexive work rivals the experience of an epiphany. What is an epiphany? To begin, an epiphany is an extraordinary experience that many people—including many or perhaps most original thinkers—never encounter at all. It may be useful to begin with a generic definition, and then reverse the usual order by providing examples, before defining an epiphany as the concept applies to reflexive work.

The Greek origins of the term epiphany refer to a manifestation or a striking appearance of some kind.[12] The term acquired a Christian sense as the manifestation of Christ's divinity to the Magi that was celebrated as a liturgical holiday January 6 of each year. However, from the nineteenth century on, the term acquired a secular meaning as a revelation. It is in this sense that James Joyce famously made reference to epiphanies at several points in his literary work. As the preceding meanings of the term imply, an epiphany appears to an individual as a sudden insight or understanding regarding something that was not seen or understood before. This sense of immediacy will be evident in the following examples and a matter of interest in subsequent discussion. For now, this immediacy is comparable in some respects to the sudden remembrance of childhood memories experienced by the narrator in Proust's *In Search of Lost Time* (see discussion of mental peripatetics in chapter 4). At one moment the narrator was unable to associate the taste of the madeleine cookie and a sip of tea with a specific situation from his childhood. At the next moment not only had he instantaneously associated the taste with a pleasurable Sunday morning ritual with his aunt, but also a montage of childhood scenes suddenly came to mind. Epiphanies arrive with the same feeling of suddenness. However, an epiphany is a sense of understanding rather than a recollection.

12. I have consulted the *Online Etymology Dictionary* for information on the origin of the term epiphany. http://www.etymonline.com/index.php?term=epiphany, accessed August 24, 2011, at 3:45 p.m.

So how then does this generic sense of epiphany apply to work or reflexive projects? Let me present two examples, one ancient and perhaps apocryphal regarding Archimedes, the highly original Greek scientist and mathematician, the other an autobiographical report by Thomas Kuhn. According to the story of Archimedes,[13] which many people consider as emblematic of an epiphany regardless of whether or not they actually use the term, in the third century BC, King Hiero of Syracuse contracted with a goldsmith to manufacture a crown. For this purpose he gave the goldsmith a precise quantity of gold. When the completed crown was presented, the king began to doubt whether the goldsmith had used the entire amount of gold he had been given. Having no wish to melt the crown in order to retrieve the gold, the King assigned Archimedes, who resided in Syracuse, to arrive at a means of determining the amount of gold while leaving the crown intact. The problem had Archimedes baffled for a time, and he gave it much thought. Then comes the emblematic bathtub epiphany. Archimedes noticed that upon entering a bathtub that was filled to the rim, the amount of water that flowed out of the tub equaled the volume of his body. It suddenly came to him that by using this method to determine the crown's volume, then by dividing the mass of the crown by the volume as thus measured he could determine the amount of gold the crown contained, as the density of gold differed from that of other metals. Archimedes was so excited by this flash of insight that he left his tub and ran through the streets (naked according to many accounts) exclaiming "Eureka! Eureka!" ("I have found it! I have found it!"). And in the end, using Archimedes's technique, it was determined that the goldsmith had indeed withheld some of the King's gold.

13. Several versions of the story are available at a website developed by the Department of Mathematics at NYU: http://www.math.nyu.edu/-corres/Archimedes/Crown/Vituvious.html, accessed August 10, 2011 at 3:00 p.m.

"Eureka!" may forever be the shorthand term for a scientific epiphany. But whether Archimedes ever uttered the term, let alone ran naked through the streets of Syracuse shouting the term, will never by truly known. It is extremely valuable, then, to have Thomas Kuhn's account of his own epiphanies as they arise when he is working on the solution to philosophical problems. Readers should note that the following passage extends the quotation from Kuhn on how he does historical work that appeared several pages back in this chapter. As the following excerpt begins, Kuhn has just completed the account quoted earlier in this chapter in which he describes the ways in which various predicaments in historical writing compel the historian to circle back to expand or reconstruct earlier passages in a work so that further progress can be made. Just before the following passage begins, Kuhn suggests that when he composes an article in philosophy, the periods of circling back are even more frequent and intense than in historical work. But there is a dramatic difference in how he prepares to write a philosophical article as opposed to an historical piece, and, for Kuhn (1977, p. 9) epiphanies play a vital role.

> But . . . what comes before the actual writing of philosophy is altogether distinct. . . . There is nothing like the historian's period of preparatory research; in the literal sense there is in most of philosophy no equivalent for research at all. One starts with a problem and a clue to its solution, both often encountered in the criticism of the work of some other philosopher. One worries it—on paper, in one's head in discussions with colleagues—waiting for the point at which it will feel ready to be written down. More often than not that feeling proves mistaken and the worrying process begins again, until the article is finally born. To me, at least, that is what

it feels like, as though the article had come to me all at once, not seriatim like the pieces of an historical narrative.

Only in the final sentence of this passage does Kuhn make clear the vital role that epiphanies play in his philosophical work. True, he never uses the term epiphany, nor for that matter, the terms revelation, or flash of understanding, or insight. Nevertheless, what he does describe—the emergence of the entire article all at once in his head—certainly qualifies as an epiphany in most secular definitions of the term. As if to underscore the sudden onset of a full-fledged work, Kuhn emphasizes that nothing happened seriatim, that is, he did not produce any line of development step by step. Unlike Archimedes, Kuhn doesn't seem startled by his sudden grasp of an elusive problem. There is no hint of any urge to shout "eureka!" while streaking through the streets. Nonetheless, in terms of intellectual processes, their experiences seem the same.

No doubt, many great philosophical works have been composed without the help of epiphanies. For example, it seems difficult to imagine that the substance and organization of *Critique of Pure Reason* simply coalesced in Immanuel Kant's mind one day. But the fact that epiphanies do occur, that certain people working on difficult problems and projects do see their way from terminus a quo to terminus ad quem poses a problem for the account of the step-by-step contextual reflexivity in the development of loosely structured projects that I have been presenting during the course of this chapter. The problem is as simple as it is obvious: if the line of development for a project can occur to an individual in an instant, then all this business about the step-by-step unfolding of contextualized development is merely a second-best option to which individuals resort if they lack the susceptibility for epiphanies that some rare confluence of biography, genetics, cultural position, and the demands of the historical era bestows upon a fortunate individual. In this sense, the fact that epiphanies really do strike some individuals supports a theory of creative genius. If you are gifted in the right way then epiphanies will come. If no epiphanies come over a long period of time, then perhaps you should consider a less challenging kind of work. This reasoning is hardly foolproof. As the previously mentioned example of Kant suggests, perhaps epiphanies may be sufficient but not necessary to the production of great projects. Perhaps step-by-step developments have virtues of their own. But still there is a puzzle about epiphanies. How does the full solution to a problem, the whole line from step one to the last item in the conclusion, come to an individual out of nowhere, as it were? Or is there more work that goes into an epiphany than dictionary definitions and the occasional shout of "eureka!" suggest?

Though a great deal about the way epiphanies emerge has yet to be investigated, I want to suggest that epiphanies have longer gestation periods involving more effort than the seemingly instantaneous appearance to the individual would make it seem. A significant item both in the story of Archimedes and Kuhn's first-person report is that in both instances thinkers found themselves at a loss for how to proceed for a certain period of time before their epiphanies arrived. Of more importance is how they spent this time. The duration and effort that precede epiphanies is clearly evident in Kuhn's close observations of his own mental processes. Having committed himself to solving a problem with only a bare minimum of clues that point a way forward, Kuhn describes a process of intense "worrying" in search of a solution, very often by himself, until he feels ready to write up his thoughts. Frequently, the effort comes up short and he begins "worrying" again. The duration of time consumed in this process is obvious, but what kind of worrying is going on here and how does it culminate in an epiphany?

Kuhn's worrying almost certainly involves intensely concentrated and highly focused efforts to solve the problem at hand. His description of worrying things out on paper and in his head suggests that more sequential and reflexive processes are at work than the immediacy of an epiphany would seem to imply. In my sense of the term these bouts of worrying are forms of solitary action. But the epiphany itself still arrives suddenly, presumably catching Kuhn, like Archimedes, by surprise. There is no action here. The epiphany is sui generis; no line of development unfolding step by step is involved.

How can this be? How can an epiphany emerge as if it were a full-fledged vision yet to be preceded by an intense period of unsuccessful thought? An imperfect but instructive analogy presents itself from the madeleine episode in Proust's *In Search of Lost Time*. Recall the episode: Proust's narrator, having vaguely recognized something nostalgic and pleasurable in the taste of the madeleine, makes several concerted attempts to associate the taste with recollections from earlier periods in his life. But all of these efforts come up empty. Now, thoroughly frustrated, the narrator decides to shift his attention to other things. But as he relaxes his concentration, suddenly memories flood his mind, first of the madeleine his aunt gave him on Sunday morning, and then, in an instant, his childhood home, scenes of his doings in his town, and more. Now, the analogy is imperfect because a sudden flood of memories is not an epiphany in the full sense of the term. Memories selectively retrieve, frame, and sometimes selectively alter impressions of experiences from the past. Epiphanies suddenly move forward tracing a path that carries the individual to some previously unattainable insight or understanding. Nevertheless, despite the difference, similar processes seem to be at work: intense but unsuccessful periods of concentrated mental activity are followed by a sudden realization. The failure of concerted activity is followed by the effortless satisfaction of success.

If this process is correct, then there must be a connection between the failure of intense concentration and the subsequent revelation. Culture, of course, plays a part in this connection. If Archimedes had been an illiterate shepherd or Kuhn knew nothing of modern academic philosophy, then they would be unprepared to launch a quest, let alone understand an epiphany as to how to arrive at their desired ends. But cultural background in itself does not connect the hard but unsuccessful work of deep thought with the sudden moment of complete insight. Here is how that connection may come about. The concerted efforts may fail, but they provide a good deal of negative information, that is, bits and pieces of knowledge about pitfalls, confusions, quandaries, inconsistencies, dead ends, and so on that arise if one tries to solve a problem or unfold whatever line of development a project of a different kind may entail. In effect, these efforts resemble falsifications in scientific research. One may not know the truth, but one has actively ruled out many possibilities. This, of course, doesn't explain the onset of the sudden revelation. No doubt that has something to do with the workings of unconscious cognition about which we know much less than we will at some future time. But it very well may be that when we do know more about the unconscious, we will discover that the hard work of failed but active reflexive thought makes a significant contribution to the epiphany that follows. In other words, an epiphany may not be a form of solitary action in itself, but it is solitary activity, frustrated though it may be, that may lay the groundwork for the effortless revelation.

REFLEXIVE PROJECTS IN EXTREME ORDEALS: SOLITARY STRUGGLES TO AVOID ANOMIE

Reflexive work makes many demands. On some occasions even the most tireless individual may grow weary from the time and energy consumed in attending to problems and predicaments of all kinds: oversights, errors, ellipses, inconsistencies, bad judgments, dead ends, and so on. Just why any given individual stays the course is difficult to say. Those who are employed may want to hold and advance in their jobs (or achieve the security of a tenured position); others may vie for public recognition or seek to influence their peers; and some may have deep moral, intellectual, or personal commitments. More likely than not, admixtures of different motives at different times keep individuals moving ahead in the face of adversity. But in one set of circumstances, as exceptional as it is extreme, individuals seek out reflexive projects, no matter how simple or difficult they may be, because the adversities with which they must deal are far more daunting than the challenges of producing a contextually reflexive pattern of any kind.

Such adversities are imposed on individuals imprisoned in solitary confinement and the challenge they confront is how to stave off the calamitous psychological effects of prolonged anomie. By anomie, I do not mean the condition attendant to the collapsing structures of normative regulation that is how Durkheim's analysis of the causes of spikes in the rates of anomic suicide is commonly understood. The condition of anomie at issue here has a closer affinity with the conditions of anomie that Harold Garfinkel (1963) investigated in his so-called breaching studies. In a variety of mundane settings Garfinkel (1963, p. 189) set out to disrupt everyday routines to the point where he induced transient moments of anomic confusion. Though

Garfinkel's studies differed from one another quite a bit, as did the reactions of his subjects to anomic situations, it is a matter of theoretical interest, as John Heritage (1984, p. 98) would later point out, that despite Garfinkel's best efforts to place subjects in disorderly and disorienting environments, his subjects generally failed to succumb to the effects of anomie. Subjects who we might have anticipated to be stunned with suspension of normal conditions of reality were rarely at a complete loss. By various means in different situations, subjects found ways to preserve some kind of order, even if the sense of order they generated mattered only to themselves.

In Heritage's sense then, one of the lessons of Garfinkel's experiments is the apparently deep-seated impulse to resist the psychic chaos that anomic conditions threaten to induce. This is not to say that resistance inevitably succeeds. It is well known that anomic conditions during times of war or following natural catastrophes cause some individuals to succumb to mental collapse from which they never fully recover.[14] Nor is this to say anything at all about how people threatened by the consequences of anomie manage to keep their sense of order. But in certain situations of solitary confinement one of the most effective ways of doing things seems to be to embark upon reflexive projects, no matter how trivial such projects might ordinarily appear to be.

Extended periods of solitary confinement present the challenge of resisting anomically induced disorientation of a dramatically different magnitude than anything a researcher such as Garfinkel might have arranged. Indeed, aside from an overriding

14. One of the most disturbing elements of the disruption of social routines is the individual's inability to determine at what point order will be restored. The phenomenon of indeterminate waiting, and the various strategies people employ to cope with this phenomenon are the subject of new investigations by Lilia Raileanu (in progress).

need to segregate an individual for the protection of others, the sole purpose of the exercise would appear to be the punitive and/ or coercive effects that isolated detention may have on the imprisoned individual. Some of the anomic effects of solitary confinement arise from a lack of social contact and interaction. However, interaction in some limited forms is not always lacking. This is especially true for political prisoners who are often kept in solitary confinement in order to induce them to disclose information or to extract confessions to the (often trumped up) accusations made against them during periodic interviews. Prisoners, of course, might find this sort of contact as oppressive as being left alone. Be this as it may, solitary confinement almost always is explicitly intended to make it as difficult as possible for prisoners to remain engaged in activities of any kind. Whereas prisoners in general may be permitted to keep reading and writing materials, playing cards, and other items that may keep them engrossed in their cells, prisoners in solitary confinement generally are denied items that they might use to occupy their minds. Matters are often made worse when prisoners are deprived of any of the usual indicators of time (e.g., lights permanently left on with no daylight in sight). Prisoners are deprived of a sense of place when they are abducted at night or placed in blindfolds while being delivered to prison. Adding further to the disorienting environmental conditions, solitary confinement suspends all but the most rudimentary daily routines. Meals may appear at standard intervals, guard shifts may change in a regular manner, but otherwise prisoners have no intrinsic everyday structure for the extended periods that they are confined to their cells.

Given these deliberately disorienting conditions, prisoners are thrown back on their own resources in order to provide for their mental stability. But, as we learn from the memoirs of individuals formerly imprisoned on political grounds, the impulse to resist anomic conditions may take the form of ingenious, disciplined, and imaginative reflexive projects developed as lines of thought exclusively within the prisoner's mind. Such projects involve prisoners in attempts to create a patch of mental order in the midst of external chaos, to make something focus the attention where nothing exists.

Consider the recollection of Terry Waite, a representative of the Church of England, who in 1987 found himself imprisoned in Lebanon, where he endured several years in solitary confinement. Waite (1995, p. 1) was keenly aware of the dangers of succumbing to the effects of anomie. Therefore he reports:

> I tried not to allow my mind to drift into despair. First, I would say my prayers, and then select a topic to think about or dream about. Often I would imagine I was about to sail around the world. I would provision my boat with everything I considered necessary, then set sail.

Another prisoner in solitary confinement, Jacobo Timmerman, who was incarcerated by extremist Argentinean government authorities in the 1970s, reports a similar exercise in creating and developing an imaginary mental reflexive project. Timmerman (1981, pp. 35–37) recognized the destructive dangers posed by random thoughts about his family, his situation, and his ultimate fate. To prevent these dangerous thoughts and memories from surfacing, Timmerman reports (1981, p. 35): "I behaved as if my mind were occupied with infinite diverse tasks. Concrete, specific tasks, chores." He did not always succeed and sometimes the thoughts of the whereabouts and situation of his family as well as the uncontrollable and unknowable nature of his future in prison got the best of him. But often he succeeded. In one instance he embarked upon writing a book in his mind.

He also devised plans to organize a bookstore. A particularly impressive feat from the standpoint of contextual reflexivity was when Timmerman (1981, pp. 84–85) cast himself as what he called a "blind architect," painstakingly putting together over a long period of time a finely detailed mental image of the exterior construction of the building in which he was being held. Timmerman was quite clever in his systematic methods. He brought to his project a background knowledge of building design, and he gathered information by observations he made from his cell and from rooms where he was taken to be tortured and interrogated. Reasoning and factual research thus allowed him to infer an image, step by step, much as a scientist might work in discovering a new atomic element, or in the manner of a painter composing a unified picture brushstroke by brushstroke, which brought diverse items together.

How did projects like these help Waite and Timmerman and other prisoners to survive their ordeals? These projects worked for them in much the same way as if they were writing a novel, conducting scientific or historical research, or debugging a poorly written computer program. As is true of these endeavors and for reflexive projects at large, once an individual begins a project, she finds herself engrossed in building a contextually integrated order, a consistent set of patterns with a focusing objective or goal. From a cognitive standpoint it takes as much concentrated involvement to select the items in sufficient quantity for an imaginary sea voyage around the world as it does to collect, collate, and organize historical data. Similarly, it takes the same mental discipline to infer from obscure bits of evidence the exterior construction of a prison building as it does to paint a closely observed still life or landscape. Moreover, especially in the case of Timmerman the "blind architect," it seems likely that there were many quandaries and predicaments along the way, moments when evidence contradicted the imaginary design and it was necessary to circle back and reconstruct earlier parts of the plan so that work could move ahead. To the author, the scientist, or the software engineer, such moments may be the kinds of frustrations one must learn to endure in order to complete a challenging project. But for prisoners in solitary confinement, matters may be different. For them, solving problems more likely is a welcome task. Indeed, building a small field of personally structured mental order in the midst of an environment in which there is no order at all is what sustained these men. Even a meaningless project allows the mind to exercise its powers of structuration, a sense of focus and efficacy that conditions of solitary confinement are meant to deny. In such conditions, making something out of nothing is one way to survive.

Chapter 6

Epilogue: Three Islands of Solitude

THREE ISLANDS OF SOLITUDE

At the close of this book a curious reader might want to know how I have managed to expand for so long on the nature and forms of solitary action without so much as passing a glance at solitude. The short explanation is that despite their shared etymological root,[1] solitary action and solitude are two very different things. This much can already be inferred from basic definitions: solitary action refers to behavior while solitude refers to a condition. Moreover, solitary action rarely extends for long periods of time. No one expects to play solitaire for a few weeks straight. Even Stakhanovites of student discipline seldom review more than a week before exams. Though authors and artists have been known to work continuously for long periods until they complete a given project, more often they keep a daily routine that alternates between solitary work and sociable interaction. Solitude is different. When one withdraws or retreats into solitude, one commits to spend a considerable time alone.

---

1. The Latin *solis*, which means "alone."

Solitude, however, differs from solitary action in a much deeper sense, and a sense that explains why a discussion of solitude only appears as an epilogue rather than an integral part of this book. Simply put, solitude is far more concerned with intense experiences than is solitary action. Even composers of extravagantly emotional music, such as Tchaikovsky's symphonies or Verdi's Requiem, must keep their feelings in check so that they can reflexively build their musical contexts by attending dispassionately to their craft. Individuals engaged in engrossments such as solitaire, crossword puzzles, or slot machines typically enjoy having their attention focused and diverted by the activity in which they are engaged. This diverting effect is the main reason why people turn to engrossments in moments of mild distress. What of peripatetics? Doesn't the nature walker or the urban flâneur seek out novel and interesting experiences? True enough, but such feelings are not necessarily very intense. One may take a walk in the woods and find an unusual flower here, see some forest creatures there, or simply enjoy the weather on a nice day. But such pleasures are far from the transcendent experiences of nature so eloquently reported by Henry David Thoreau in his account of his solitary stay in a small dwelling adjacent to Walden Pond. Indeed, as we shall see, Thoreau found himself transported by nature, even in the absence of anything unusual or of particular interest at all. Other forms of solitude, though hardly pleasurable in any way whatsoever, are even more intense than Thoreau's experiences in the Massachusetts countryside. I refer here to the agonies of the true religious anchorite who feels called into solitude to find one's way to God through doubt and anguish that offer recurrent tests of faith. And I refer also to the episodes of deep distress that drive many people into solitude to absorb and manage feelings that must be experienced alone, to make sense of these feelings, and to determine how to move on from the distress.

One more thing to notice about these solitudes is that they are exceedingly rare. It takes a person with profound and unusual spiritual dedication to undertake a solitary religious vocation, and especially to stay the course. It also takes a person of unusual sensitivity and capacity to live alone, to dwell for very long in the solitude of a tranquil retreat. Personal distress is a more common experience, but most of us do not live all or most of our lives with feelings so turbulent that we feel driven to be alone. These solitudes are like islands just offshore the coast of everyday life to which people retreat when driven by intense feelings or when intense experiences beckon or call. They are situated apart from everyday life because their daily rounds of interaction and solitary action would distract or interrupt individuals from the experiences they need or seek. Moreover, with the exception of the religious anchorite, whose solitude is unique in many ways, people not only withdraw to the islands of solitude, they return from them back into society again. In this sense, it is not surprising that people who make solitary retreats write essays and poetry about their experiences. Their written works testify to the fact that they don't mean to leave society behind, once and for all.

In the following sections I shall expand on my remarks here with regard to the three realms of solitude mentioned above. I claim no categorical closure here. There may be many other realms of solitude. Nor do I offer a full introduction to each realm. That task might well entail an entire book in itself. Drawing on a few authors who seem to me to have especially acute and edifying insights, my intent here is merely to identify a sampling of the islands of solitude that lie off the coast of modern Western life.

SOLITARY RELIGIOUS VOCATIONS: SOME INSIGHTS FROM THOMAS MERTON

Those who withdraw to the monastic cell, or more often in earlier times the desert cave or the wilderness hut, enter solitude in
its most extreme form. They are, in fact, a species of what Max
Weber ([1912–1913] 1946, p. 287) memorably termed religious
virtuosi, a species marked not only by withdrawal, but by self-
imposed asceticism as well. If, as sometimes happens, solitude is
referenced with an aura of mysticism or mystery surrounding the
term, the solitude of the religious anchorite or hermit is an obvious source of the aura we detect. Saints Anthony and Jerome and
Paul of Thebes left such a deep impression on early Christian culture and such an enduring legacy in monastic orders that it may
seem anachronistic to speak of such spiritual vocations today.
True, they are rare, but then we cannot be sure how common or
rare were the solitudes of early Christianity, or for that matter,
the solitudes of pre-Christian mystics or the solitary vocations
undertaken by members of Eastern religions in the past or in
more recent times. In any event, the spiritual call to solitude has
not been completely extinguished in modern times. This much
is evident from the life of Thomas Merton (1915–1968). Late in
life Merton withdrew into solitude as a religious hermit. However, many publications from his large output of writings prior
to that point not only make clear that he felt the call to a solitary vocation, but also that he possessed a subtle understanding
and appreciation of what is at stake in the sacred pursuit and the
challenges that confront the individual who accepts this vocation. Merton's "Notes for a Philosophy of Solitude" (1960) presents one of his most thoughtful and acute examinations of the
spiritual vocation to solitude. I shall rely on Merton's insights
here as a guide to this reclusive way of life.

A number of principle themes in Merton's essays are summarized in the following passage:

The true solitary is not one who simply withdraws from society. Mere withdrawal, regression, leads to a sick solitude, without meaning and without fruit. The solitary of whom I speak is called not to leave society but to transcend it; not to withdraw from the fellowship with other men but to renounce the appearance, the myth of union in diversion in order to attain union on a higher and a more spiritual level—the mystic level of the Body of Christ. He renounces that union with his immediate neighbors which is apparently achieved through the medium of the aspirations, fictions, and conventions prevalent in his social group. But in so doing he attains to the basic, invisible, mysterious unity which makes all men "one Man" in Christ's Church beyond, and in spite of natural social groups by which their special myths and slogans keep man in a state of division. The solitary then has a mysterious and apparently absurd vocation to supernatural unity. He seeks a simple, spiritual oneness in himself which when it is found, paradoxically becomes the oneness of all men (Merton 1960, pp. 181–182).

Merton's sweeping dismissal of "mere withdrawal" underscores the qualities of Weber's religious virtuoso to which, in effect, Merton implies every true solitary must aspire. The solitary renounces the superficial "diversions" (and self-deceptions, self-gratification, social myths, illusion, and even the kind of simple faith that prevails among Christians in everyday life), as Merton makes clear at various points in the essay. The solitary seeks a mystical, mysterious union with the divine, but a union he experiences within himself as an oneness with all humanity as well. There is what Merton calls an absurd quality in this quest, but not the absurdity that might occur to the uncomprehending bystander. The absurdity comes with the solitary's "anguish of realizing that underneath the apparent logical pattern of a more or less 'well-organized' rational life there lays an abyss of rationality, confusion, pointlessness, and indeed chaos" (1960, p. 179).[2] Merton goes on to condense this interior sense of life's absurdity in a trenchant way. This absurdity involves a special kind of renunciation, a renunciation of "the seemingly harmless pleasure of building a tight self-contained illusion about himself and his little world" (Merton 1960, p. 180).

It is not out of place to notice here how far removed the ascetic renunciation of Merton's solitary is from the everyday solitary actions I have analyzed elsewhere in this book. Consider only the affinity between the building of tight self-contained illusions about oneself and one's little world that Merton suggests the solitary must renounce and the step-by-step context formation that is the axial element in solitary action. Rather than building context, at least in the early stages of a vocation the solitary must let it go, that is, abjure context formation of any kind. Merton's reference to the construction of illusion is on a grander scale than the step-by-step process of context formation at the heart of solitary action. But it is quite clear that Merton leaves no place for the individual on a spiritual vocation to follow a sequence of action as if completing a crossword puzzle or wandering peripatetically from one involving item to the next. Nor is the solitary reflexively composing a work of some kind such as a poem, a painting, or a

2. Though Merton shapes the concept of the absurd to his own purposes here, existential philosophers had devised arguments about the absurdity of human projects and human existence at least as far back as Kierkegaard and forward in more recent times up to Albert Camus and Jean-Paul Sartre, who were all widely read in Merton's time. Kierkegaard may be of special relevance here. He bridged the absurd with Christian faith in ways that provide a useful backdrop to understanding Merton's thought.

mathematical theory. The only one of the four forms of solitary action that has any bearing on the spiritual solitary's quest is the discipline of the demanding regimen, the kind of discipline that keeps a student hard at work when the lesson she must master lacks any means to produce any structure yet demands her undivided attention. But this resemblance only goes so far because the student need undertake a regimen for no more than several hours at a time for a few study sessions a week. The spiritual vocation is a continuous affair. So long as the individual persists in the quest, the self-imposed discipline is an integral aspect of daily life.

In a sense, the absurd renunciation of the construction of illusions would make it seem as though in the early stages of a solitary vocation the individual creates a condition of anomie. Indeed, Merton (1960, pp. 184–200) devotes a substantial section of his essay to what he terms a "sea of perils," many of which refer to the confusion, insecurities, and doubts that victims of solitary confinement such as Terry Anderson and Jacobo Timmerman struggled to avoid with great feats of cognitive ingenuity. Though Merton (1960, pp. 197–198) finds that certain individuals are, in a sense, destined from an early age for a solitary life and for which they may be well-suited by temperament and character, many others reach the spiritual vocation of solitude the "hard way," and it is these individuals who face the perils of what I here suggest are the effects of anomie. The torment of these experiences is described in remarkably vivid imagery toward the close of the essay when Merton (1960, p. 202) writes of the plight of the solitary who finds he cannot pray, see, or hope (Merton suggests this circumstance may not be rare). At such times the solitary individual may experience: "Not the sweet passivity which the books [that supply popular versions of solitude] extol, but a bitter, arid struggle to press forward through a blinding sandstorm. The solitary may beat his head against the wall of doubt. That may be the full extent of his contemplation . . . a doubt that undermines his very reasons for existing and for doing what he does."

Nowhere in everyday life will one encounter the extraordinary struggle of the spiritual vocation. Indeed, Merton's candor about the perils of the solitary spiritual quest seem intended to disabuse those who might have romantic notions about the pleasures of this extraordinary, intense, and trying way of life. But the vocation, of course, is not about asceticism and the renunciation of mundane illusions. It is rather about the transcendent experience of unity with God and humanity. Here Merton (1960, p. 202), as befits a religious mystic, leaves us with a mystery. The tortuous existential doubt ultimately ends in silence, and with silence comes an end to all existential questions. But when the questions end, a spiritual certitude arrives, "the only certitude he knows: The presence of God in the midst of uncertainty, and nothingness." This experience is so distant, even from the lives of the devout laity, that to frame this reception of certainty in the divine as a matter of sociological interest necessarily and inevitably misses the point. And, indeed, there is no way forward here for the sociology of solitary action. The experience of spiritual certitude may arrive like an epiphany of the kind considered at the end of chapter 5.[3] But what comes then? Merton (pp. 202–203)

3. Simone Weil, a deeply spiritual essayist, suggests the possibility that both science and art may in rare instances be undertaken as sacred (or perhaps, quasi-sacred solitary quests):

> Truth and beauty dwell on this level of the impersonal and the anonymous. This is the realm of the sacred. . . . What is sacred in science is truth; what is sacred in art is beauty. Truth and beauty are impersonal . . . impersonality is only reached by the practice of a form of attention which is rare in itself, and impossible except in solitude, and not only physical but mental solitude (Weil [1950] 1977, p. 318).

Weil, of course, means to refer here only to the heroic artist or the scientific genius. The mystical sense of the truth and beauty to which she refers perhaps alludes to the kind of epiphany discussed in chapter 5.

tells us: "the solitary man says nothing, does his work. . . . He knows where he is going, but he is not sure of his way."

Though Merton's way is by no means an authoritative account of the Christian solitary vocation, and I have not even touched upon Buddhist, Hindu, or other solitary spiritual quests, his account has an existential ring of truth. And to the extent that it does, it is evident that the activities in sacred, solitary quests have trajectories and outcomes unlike solitary actions of any other kind. This is indeed the solitude of the virtuoso, and from a sociological standpoint it is sui generis in the literal sense that it is a species unto itself.

SOLITUDE AS A REFINED RETREAT

To shift from the life of sacrifice and tribulation of the religious anchorite to the temporal solitude described by poets and essayists since ancient times is to create a disjunction so sharp that it justifies in itself the need to treat solitude as a series of different realms. But there is something illusory at times about this second realm of solitude. We know of this solitude primarily because well-regarded members of literary elites have sung its praises, beginning in ancient Rome. More to the point, most of these authors employ romantic styles and voices that create ornately stylized images of a kind of carefree solitude that seems too good to be true. A reader who does not easily fall under the romantic spell of such works is led to wonder if such solitudes exist. Probably so, albeit in less exalted ways. There have likely always been some folks, who, like Montaigne ([1572–1574] 1958, Ch. 39)—an essayist who goes out of his way to maintain a credible and balanced voice—have opted to retire from public life to enjoy time by themselves reading and enjoying the fine fruits of a life well lived. But the pool of people prepared to live this life must be small. For one thing, people must possess the financial resources to support themselves or the full set of skills necessary to live off the land. For another, they must possess the free time to leave society behind for an extended period of time. Moreover, they must possess peace of mind, a rare commodity indeed, at least in our anxious and troubled times. But as Montaigne cautions readers of his essay on solitude ([1572–1575] 1958, pp. 177–178), those burdened with troublesome feelings and desires cannot enjoy this kind of solitude. In saying this, Montaigne draws a line that distinguishes this tranquil realm of solitude from the two tumultuous realms discussed above and below. Emotional turmoil seems all but inevitable in the spiritual solitude of the ascetic anchorite and the experience of turmoil is at the heart of the deeply troubled solitarist to be discussed in the next section. The solitude here is that of an individual whose mind is already relaxed.

No matter how rare the present realm of solitude is in practice, it occupies a special hold in the popular imagination today. This is because the aesthetic quality of literary accounts of this solitude has settled on an idyllic image of solitary life in nature. Beyond romantic literature, this image has grown with the advent of entire genres of paintings and photographs of beautiful landscapes and seascapes with either a solitary individual or no sign of human habitation at all. Nature itself, in effect, replaces fine books as the beauty we come to appreciate by ourselves. Nature may not be like this. But in wistful moments, no doubt, making an idyllic solitary retreat is a widely shared fond dream. A few illustrious landmarks can provide a glimpse of how this aesthetically refined image of solitude evolved.

The culturally refined connotation of solitude began with the authors who first described the practice in the later period of the history of ancient Rome. As Robert Sayre (1978, pp. 20–25) suggests, the taste for solitude emerged as land for rural second homes became available to successful public figures. Sayre does not say how popular the idea may have been, but we know it mainly through the writings of Roman authors whose influence survived their time, including Horace, Seneca, and Pliny the Younger. The following excerpt from a poem by Horace illustrates the refined sense of enjoyment in solitary retreat in its classic Roman form:

> O rural home: when shall I behold you! When shall I be able, Now with books of the ancients. Now with sleep and idles hours To quaff sweet forgetfulness of life's cares (Horace in Sayre 1978, p. 22).

The Roman idea of solitude resurfaces much closer to modern times. One of the best expressions of this continuation comes in the "Ode on Solitude," by Alexander Pope, who may have written it at a very precocious age.[4] Be this as it may, it is worth mentioning that Pope was a lifelong student of ancient Roman poetry, ultimately composing a set of works entitled "Imitations of Horace" (1733–1738). It may be that Pope's "Ode on Solitude" may thus directly expand upon Horace's Roman appreciation of solitude:

> Happy the man, whose wish and care
> A few paternal acres bound,
> Content to breathe his native air,
> In his own ground.
> Whose herds with mil, whose fields with bread,
> Whose flocks supply him with attire,
> Whose trees in summer yield him shade,
> In winter fire.
> Blest! Who can unconcern'dly find

---

4. The poem is dated 1700, which would mean Pope was twelve years of age.

Hours, days, and years slide soft away,
In health of body, peace of mind,
Quiet by day,
Sound sleep by night; study and ease
Together mix'd; sweet recreation,
And innocence, which most does please,
With meditation.
Thus let me live, unseen, unknown;
Thus unlamented let me dye;
Steal from the world, and not a stone
Tell where I lye.

The poetic form already suggests the refined quality of the solitary retreat. We observe as well that while Pope does not require a large estate for his solitude, he does ask for an inherited farm, a property that only prosperous English families could expect to pass along to their offspring at the time. Unlike Horace, Pope longs for the self-sufficiency that a working farm affords. But it is not at all clear that he would prefer to do any farm work himself. Instead, as in Horace, we find Pope eager for the tranquil life of alternating between periods of reading and sleep. This is not the life of an active aristocrat or businessman. It is rather an ideal for a certain kind of cultural aesthete. It is, of course, also a romanticized ideal rather than a reality. There may have been landowners with inheritances sizable enough to provide them with an abundance of leisure time. But it is doubtful, that even among this highly advantaged elite, life was as idyllic as Pope imagined it to be. The notion of solitary retreats has attracted other romantics as well. For example, as Wolfgang Lepenies ([1969] 1992, Chs. 2–3) observes, a sense of melancholy was introduced to the notion of solitary retreat in the late middle ages and early modern times. Here solitude was seen as a refuge for second-level aristocrats and bourgeois arrivistes who found themselves cut off from any real access to power. Confined to superficial rounds of social relations fleshed out with gossip and rumor in literary salons, members of this frustrated stratum found meaning in life and opportunities for emotional release in a new Romantic ideal of solitude, an ideal composed of heterogeneous elements such as the love of nature, a sensitive appreciation of literature and the fine arts, and above all, a bias in favor of emotion over reason (Lepenies [1969] 1992, p. 66).

The frustrated romantics of whom Lepenies writes may have amplified and refined the aesthetic appreciation of nature that was a more implicit than explicit quality of the classical sense of solitude as it advanced from Romans to Pope. This is not to overlook the melancholy note they also introduced, a note of sadness bordering on self-pity epitomized, if not hyperbolized, in various remarks of Jean-Jacques Rousseau in his *Reveries of the Solitary Walker* ([1776] 1979), remarks in which he laments the rejection and estrangement he felt from the literary circles whose acceptance he desired. But as we approach modern times, the romantic (or at least romantically rendered) experience of living alone in harmony with nature has flourished to a greater extent.

One can cite any number of poets, essayists, and artists who have contributed to the aesthetic appreciation of nature. But a smaller number recounted how it actually felt to withdraw into nature for a considerable period of time. One author who did, Henry David Thoreau, brought with him a literary talent, a romantic sensitivity, an aversion to town life,[5] and an abounding love of nature that makes his *Walden* a beautiful, and in some ways a seductive, statement of the small joys and tranquil pleasures of absorbing the atmosphere and the detail of encountering

5. This aversion was by no means complete. In the course of *Walden*, Thoreau mentions recurrent visits to Concord, Massachusetts, a town situated about two miles from his solitary retreat, where he had many friends.

nature by oneself. Consider only the first sentences of the section of *Walden* devoted to solitude ([1854] 1992, p. 87).

This is a delicious evening, when the whole body is one sense, and imbibes delight through every pore. I go and come with a strange liberty in Nature, a part of herself. As I walk along the stony shore of the pond in my shirtsleeves, though it is cool as well as cloudy and windy, and I see nothing special to attract me, all the elements are unusually congenial to me. The bullfrogs trump to usher in the night, and the note of the whip-poor-will is borne on the rippling wind from over the water. Sympathy with the fluttering alder and poplar leaves almost takes away my breath; yet, like the lake, my serenity is rippled but not ruffled. These small waves raised by the evening wind are as remote from storm as the smooth reflecting surface.

One can find many passages of this kind in *Walden*.[6] But one of the most interesting things about this selection and about the section of *Walden* on solitude at large ([1854] 1992, p. 87–94) is his emphasis upon serenity, which like the lake in the breeze is "riffled but not ruffled." Another selection from the section on solitude ([1954] 1992, p. 88) expands upon this peace of mind in a straightforward way:

I experienced sometimes that the most sweet and tender, the most innocent and encouraging society may be found in any natural object, even for the poor misanthrope and most melancholy man. There can be no very black melancholy to him who lives in the midst of Nature and has his senses still. There was never yet such a storm but it was Aeolian music to a healthy and innocent ear. Nothing can rightly compel a simple and

---

6. Thoreau's chapter entitled "The Pons" is especially rich.

brave man to a vulgar sadness. While I enjoy the friendship of
the seasons I trust that nothing can make life a burden to me.

Though Thoreau leaves no literary hint, it may be that he here
means to dismiss the romantic belief that solitude is a time for
melancholy or dark moods. In any event, he is quite clear about
his own peace and joy living alone in the woods. It should be said
that Thoreau did not spend all of his time simply soaking in these
good feelings. Indeed, the first chapter of *Walden* details the work
he performed on the woodland plot he occupied in return for improving the property. Thoreau also read a great deal, and he obviously wrote a great deal as well. Still, Thoreau ([1854] 1992, p. 89)
is perhaps more aware than many of his admirers that not every
individual is as fit for solitude as he.[7] This point, which echoes
Thomas Merton's sense that some are better fit than others for
the rigors of a solitary vocation, also provides an instructive contrast with the discussion that follows of solitude as distress. For,
as will be evident momentarily, those who turn to solitude with
their troubles are driven to solitude regardless of whether or not
they are well suited for the solitary life.

SOLITUDE IN TIMES OF DISTRESS

In all likelihood, circumstances of emotional distress, more than
any other condition, induce people to withdraw from interpersonal routines. Distress with this kind of power comes in many

7. There is anticipation here of an argument made by Thoreau's close friend and
fellow transcendentalist, Ralph Waldo Emerson. Emerson's "Society and Solitude"
(1870) argues that intellectually and artistically gifted individuals are unlike ordinary people in their unique need for solitude. Thoreau's writings on solitude in
Walden are much too egalitarian to support Emerson's point. Nonetheless, there is,
in many passages in *Walden*, an elitist sense of superior abilities to appreciate nature.

different forms. The prototype here is grief over the loss of a loved one. But people may also feel the need for a solitary retreat after receiving a frightening medical diagnosis, after the dissolution of an intimate relationship or the disintegration of a family, or following the trauma of being fired or otherwise suffering a severe setback in one's finances, occupation, or career. These are instances of what Anthony Giddens (1991, Ch. 4) terms "fateful moments," moments when unavoidable circumstances force life-altering choices upon individuals. It is a time when one's narrative of self-identity and relationships with others that may have been taken for granted for many years may need to be reframed, reinterpreted, and revised. Who am I now that I am a widow? Unemployed? Disabled? A victim of a life-threatening disease? Did I make good or bad choices up to now? Does my life in retrospect look different? What do I do next?

Such questions are almost inevitable in times of personal crisis. Moreover, as the late British psychotherapist Anthony Storr (1988, p. 29) observes, it is better at times for others to set aside the impulse to comfort or support the troubled until we are sure they may not prefer to be alone. There are some questions only individuals have the personal experience and capacity to answer for themselves. But matters here may be a bit less clear-cut than an inevitable drive to answer existential questions may make it appear. Some people are more adept at self-reflection than others. Some may prefer to discuss their adjustments in times of crisis with a trusted confidante or a psychotherapist. For others an alternation between such conversations and episodes of solitary reflection may work best. Thus, solitary existential reflection in troubled times is not a given but rather a varying matter of degree.

It is more difficult to discuss with others the powerful emotions that drive people in distress to be alone, regardless of whether or not existential questions arise. It is true, of course, that many non-modern cultures permit or encourage individuals who suffered great loss due to death, disaster, or war, to cry out in public their anguish, anger, and despair. But in such cultures there are few acceptable moments to express one's personal fears, remorse, or humiliation. All of this is exacerbated by the strand of individualism in modern cultures that encourages individuals to keep a poised face in public (see Goffman, 1967, Ch. 1–2) and a sense of self-discipline and restraint that Max Weber ([1905] 1958, p. 183) once famously described as "the iron cage."

Such restraints may not be confined to acute crises. Emotions such as fear, remorse, and shame may accumulate while in public, to the point where the individual withdraws into solitude to allow the feelings to emerge. These are periods of catharsis, the release of pent-up emotions. Freed from the properties of interaction, the individuals are free to absorb the brunt of their feelings without concern that they may embarrass themselves or anyone else. Having experienced their feelings, they may also try to make sense of them no matter how inconsistent or guilt provoking they may be. To vent one's feelings is seldom easy or comfortable. But, catharsis in itself is widely recognized to end up having a calming effect even if the source of the painful feelings will always remain in view.

What is it about catharsis that offers emotional relief? The conventional answer, and the persuasive one as well, is that people simply need to purge their feelings much as a steam kettle whistles to permit the pent-up steam to escape. But perhaps catharsis offers comfort in another way as well. Anthony Storr (1988, p. 31) describes a folk theory held in some parts of rural Greece; the local custom requires widows to withdraw form society for five years before returning to their regular social life. The rural Greeks hold that by recurrently feeling the loss (e.g., during daily visits to the husband's grave) the widow experiences her grief many times over until she has absorbed it to the point where she dulls her pain and then comes to terms with it in her life. Though five uninterrupted years of grief may be more time apart from society than most people can bear, recurrent periods of solitude may help people to manage all kinds of distressing feelings, some chronic and others acute. It may take many nights alone in bed before one begins to diminish the pitch and frequency of the waves of fear stirred up by a threatening medical diagnosis. Likewise, exceptionally self-critical individuals may need to withdraw periodically to bank the fires of self-reproach in the ashes of regret.

Such is the case for May Sarton, a talented, and in the late stages of her career, a widely acclaimed poet and novelist. She was also a person with the courage to expose her deepest criticism of herself in print, and though her candid and dignified voice speaks well for her, her self-criticisms were often painful and harsh. Though Sarton led a very busy social life, complete with travel, friendship, and love,[8] to accommodate her feelings she periodically retreated by herself to a small house she kept for the purpose, first in New Hampshire and then in Maine. In 1973 she published a memoir of one of these visits entitled *Journal of a Solitude*, which is one of the best examples I have seen of catharsis put into words. Consider several lines from the opening entry in the book:

> For a long time now, every meeting with another human being has been a collision. I feel too much, sense too much, exhausted by the reverberations after even the simplest

8. For more on May Sarton's life see Leonora Blouin, "May Sarton: A Poet's Life." This piece appears on a site devoted to "A Celebration of Women Writers" hosted at the University of Pennsylvania.

conversation. But the deep collision is and has been with my unregenerate, tormenting and tormented self. . . . I feel like an inadequate machine that breaks down at crucial moments and grinds to a dreadful halt . . . or, even worse, explodes in some innocent person's face. . . . I live alone, perhaps for no good reason, for the reason that I am an impossible creature set apart by a temperament I have never learned to use as it could be used, thrown off by a word, a glance, a rainy day, or one drink too many. My need to be alone is balanced against my fear of what will happen when I enter the huge, empty silence if I cannot find support there. I go up to heaven and down to hell in an hour (Sarton, 1973, p. 12).

Sarton provides in other entries more specific events she regrets, along with commentaries on her worries and anxieties. She knows herself well enough to know that she has an "impossible" temperament. So, while she does strive to make sense of her feelings, one does not get the sense that she is engaged in some kind of self-therapy. It appears more likely that Sarton needs these times alone in rural New England to simply absorb feelings of the burdens of being with other people, of the harms she feels she has inflicted on some, and for her own continuing dissatisfaction with herself. Unlike the widow, or the newly divorced, or the fired, Sarton can never come to grips with these feelings once and for all. Her recurrent retreats are better understood as episodes when she allows herself to register and recognize her feelings about herself for what they are. Though she wrestles with her sense that she must try to improve, it also seems that by releasing the full force of her feelings she is able to keep them from overwhelming her as well. Thus, Sarton's solitudes are the way she copes with her emotions and this, in turn, enables her to return from solitude with the ability to fully engage in her social life again. As in the Greek folk theory, she enters her solitudes to rehearse feelings she already knows well. Perhaps she found these episodes necessary to absorb, and then through repetition, to dull the cutting edge of her self-criticism, and thereby dull her self-inflicted pain.

AN INTERSECTION BETWEEN SOLITUDE
AND SOLITARY ACTION

Many cultures have devised forms of solitude beyond the three I have mentioned here. One thinks immediately of Buddhist practices of silent meditation, but there are many others besides.[9] Analyzing such solitude would require another, very different book. But one intersection between all forms of solitude on the one hand and solitary action as discussed in the main body of this book on the other deserves at least a few words here. As those subject to solitary confinement attest, being alone for long periods of time can be a dangerous thing. So how do those driven or called into solitude cope with this danger? Jacobo Timmerman and Terry Anderson coped by developing, in their minds, complicated reflexive projects, piece by piece. But those who live in the forms of solitude identified above do not have the mental latitude for such cognitively demanding tasks. They are too absorbed in their experiences, the spiritual tribulations of the anchorite, the intense pleasure of the refined retreat, and the turbulent catharsis and personal adjustment of those who withdraw into solitude in times of distress. Living with such intense experiences by oneself can be almost intolerable without some crutch to lean on while alone.

9. For an interesting study of one form of Buddhist solitude see Pagis (2010).

One can only speculate on what that crutch might be. Some undoubtedly rely on prescribed medications or other kinds of drugs. But one consistent thread in my readings on solitude suggests another type of crutch as well. The dangers of anomie in solitude here can be relieved by the regimens of daily routines. Recall here Bernice Martin's account of housework as "magic," discussed in chapter 2. Martin found that she could manage her own daily troubles through her routine of household chores. Closer to the point at hand, Martin also recounts the story of her friend suffering from life-threatening cancer, who insisted on cleaning her own bathroom according to her lifelong routine, as taught to her by her mother. Like Martin, the friend found comfort in performing what amounted to mindless tasks, yet tasks that took discipline and a certain kind of attention to detail.

Perhaps it is not coincidental then that the main sources for the realms of solitude I have discussed here include some references to steady work of a routine kind. Merton, as I have mentioned briefly above, advises those on a solitary vocation to keep to their daily work even as they remain uncertain of where they are bound. Thoreau, as also noted above, devotes an entire chapter to the work he did while he was alone at Walden. But May Sarton (1973, p. 84) brings the routine of regimented solitary action into solitude in a particularly vivid way that supports Bernice Martin's insights, albeit, as the character of Sarton's descriptions of her solitary swirls of feelings suggest, with a stronger accent on the discipline and the pain. In some ways her sense of imprisonment and her management of chaos is also reminiscent of Timmerman and Anderson. But there are no reflexive intellectual gymnastics here. Sarton writes instead of what she (1973, pp. 83–84) terms "inexorable structure" of her "usual days."

[A]s a prisoner does (and in winter my life is imprisoned much of the time), I know it is essential for me to move within a structure. The bed must be made (it is what I hate doing most), the dishes washed, the place tidied up before I can get to work [her writing] with a free mind. There must be rewards for hard tasks, and often a cigarette had been the reward for putting out the rubbish or cleaning [her pet bird's] cage. In the winter when I cannot garden, I make an effort to get the chaos behind closed doors.

And so by way of May Sarton's regimens, we find that even those in the most anguished conditions of solitude bring along some forms of solitary action to keep their lives and their minds in order. As the examples of Timmerman and Anderson illustrate, in some situations reflexives serve this purpose as well. And we should not forget the millions of people with time on their hands that play solitaire, work on jigsaw puzzles, or get caught up in other engrossments each day. Solitude may be a rare condition, but regimens, reflexives, peripatetics and engrossments are as ubiquitous as interaction, and even in the deep experiences of solitude, just as necessary to our everyday well-being.

BIBLIOGRAPHY

Airês, Phillip, and Duby, Georges. 1987–1991. *A History of Private Life*. 4 volumes. Translated by Arthur Goldhammer. Cambridge, MA: Harvard University Press.

Andrade, Jackie. 2009.Published online at http:/onlinelibrary.wiley.com/doi/10.1002/acp/1561/abstract. Accessed August 21, 2012.

Archer, Margaret S. 2003. *Structure, Agency and the Internal Conversation*. Cambridge, UK: Cambridge University Press.

Arendt, Hannah. 1977. *The Life of the Mind*. New York: Harcourt Brace.

Aristotle. 1981. *The Politics: Revised Edition*. Translated by A. E. Sinclair. Revised by T. J. Saunders. New York: Penguin.

Baker, Nicholson. *Room Temperature: A Novel*. 1984. New York: Random House.

Blouin, Leonora. "May Sarton: A Poet's Life." Online at a Celebration of Women Writers. University of Pennsylvania at http://digital.library.upenn.edu/women/sarton/blouin-biogrphy.html. Accessed July 17, 2012.

Campbell, Colin. 1996. *The Myth of Social Action*. Cambridge, UK: Cambridge University Press.

Cohen, Ira J. 1989. *Structuration Theory: Anthony Giddens and the Constitution of Social Life*. London and New York: Macmillan.

Cohen, Ira J., and Rogers, Mary F. 1994. "Autonomy and Credibility: Voice as Method." *Sociological Theory* 12 (3): pp. 304–318.

Coleman, James S. 1990. *Foundations of Social Theory*. Cambridge, MA: Harvard University Press.

Csikszentmihalyi, Mihaly. 1990. Flow: *The Psychology of Optimal Experience*. New York: Harper and Row.

Damasio, Antonio. 1999. *The Feeling of What Happens: Body and Emotions in the Making of Consciousness*. New York: Harvester.

Defoe, Daniel. [1719] 2003. *Robinson Crusoe*. New York: Barnes and Noble.

Department of Mathematics, New York University. "Archimedes Home Page." Published online at http:/www.math.nyu.edu/~crorres/Archimedes/contents.html. Accessed August 22, 2012.

Dewey, John. 1922. *Human Nature and Conduct*. New York: Holt and Company.

DiCicco-Bloom, B. and Gibson, David R. 2010. "More than a Game: Sociological Theory from the Theories of Games." *Sociological Theory* 28: pp. 247–271.

DiMaggio, Paul. 1997. "Culture and Cognition." *Annual Review of Sociology* 23: pp. 263–287.

Durkheim, Emile. [1895] 1982. *Rules of Sociological Method*. Translated by W. D. Hall. New York: Free Press.

Durkheim, Emile. [1897] 1951. *Suicide: A Study in Sociology*. Translated by John A. Spaulding and George Simpson. New York: Free Press.

Durkheim, Emile. [1898] 1973. "Individualism and the Intellectuals." Translated by Mark Traugott. Edited by Robert Bellah, pp. 43–60. In *Emile Durkheim on Morality and Society*. Chicago: University of Chicago Press.

Edelman, Gerald M. 2006. *Second Nature: Brain Science and Human Knowledge*. New Haven, CT: Yale University Press.

Emerson, Ralph Waldo. 1870. *Society and Solitude*. Boston, MA: Fields, Osgood.

Evans, Jonathan St. B. 2008. "Dual-Processing Accounts of Reasoning, Judgment, and Social Cognition." *Annual Review of Psychology* 59: pp. 259–278.

Faulkner, R. and Becker, Howard S. 2009. *Do You Know? The Jazz Repertoire in Action*. Chicago: University of Chicago Press.

Foucault, Michel. [1975] 1977. *Discipline and Punish: The Birth of the Prison*. Translated by Alan Sheridan. New York: Random House.

Frankl, Viktor E. 1984. *Man's Search for Meaning*. New York: Simon and Schuster.

Garfinkel, Harold. 1963. "A Conception of, and Experiments with, 'Trust': As a Condition of Stable Concerted Actions." In *Motivation and Interaction*. Edited by O. J. Harvey, pp. 187–238. New York: Ronald Press.

Garfinkel, Harold. 1967. *Studies in Ethnomethodology*. Englewood Cliffs, NJ: Prentice Hall.

Garfinkel, Harold. 1988. "Evidence for Locally Produced, Naturally Accountable Phenomena of Order*, Logic, Reason, Meaning, Method, Etc., in and as of the Essential Quiddity of Immortal Society, (I of IV): An Announcement of Studies." *Sociological Theory* 6 (1): pp. 203–209.

Garfinkel, Harold. 2002. *Ethnomethodology's Program: Working Out Durkheim's Aphorism.* Edited by Anne Warfield Rawls. Latham, MD: Rowman and Littlefield.

Garfinkel, Harold. 2006. "Respecifying the Study of Social Order—Garfinkel's Transition from Theoretical Conceptualization to Practices in Details." In *Seeing Sociologically: The Routine Grounds of Social Action*, edited by Anne Warfield Rawls, pp. 1–97. Boulder, CO: Paradigm Press.

Garfinkel, Harold. 2006. *Seeing Sociologically: The Routine Grounds of Social Action.* Edited by Anne Warfield Rawls. Philadelphia, PA: Temple University Press.

Garfinkel, Harold; Lynch, Michael; Livingston, Eric. 1981. "The Work of Discovering Science with Materials Construed with Materials from Optically Discovered Pulsar." *Philosophy of Social Sciences* 11: pp. 131–158.

Garfinkel, Harold. Sacks, Harvey. 1970. "On Formal Structures of Practical Actions." In *Theoretical Sociology.* Edited by L. C. McKinney and E. A. Tiryakin, pp. 338–366. New York: Appleton-Croft.

Giddens, Anthony. 1979. *Central Problems in Social Theory: Action, Structure and Contradiction in Social Theory.* London: Macmillan.

Giddens, Anthony. 1984. *The Constitution of Society: Outline of the Theory of Structuration.* Cambridge, UK: Polity Press.

Giddens, Anthony. 1991. *Modernity and Self-Identity: Self and Society in the Late Modern Age.* Cambridge, England: Polity Press.

Goffman, Erving. 1963. *Behavior in Public Places: Notes on the Social Organization of Gatherings.* New York: Free Press.

Goffman, Erving. 1967. *Interaction Ritual Essays on Face-to-Face Behavior.* New York: Pantheon.

Goffman, Erving. 1971. *Relations in Public: Microstudies.* New York: Basic Books.

Goffman, Erving. 1974. *Frame Analysis: An Essay on the Organization of Experience.* New York: Harper.

Goffman, Erving. "The Interaction Order." 1983. *American Sociological Review* 48 (1) February, pp. 1–17.

Guenther, Lisa. 2012. "The Living Death of Solitary Confinement." *The New York Times*, August 26. http://opinionator.blogs.nytimes.com/2012/08/26/the-living-death-of-solitary confinement/. Accessed August 26, 2012.

Heritage, John. 1984. *Garfinkel and Ethnomethodology.* Cambridge, UK: Polity.

Hobbes, Thomas. [1651] 1968. *On the Citizen (De Civis).* Cambridge, UK: Cambridge University Press.

Hobbes, Thomas. [1647] 1998. *Leviathan.* Harmondsworth, UK: Penguin.

Hochschild, Arlie Russell. 1979. "Emotion Work, Feeling Rules, and Social Structure." *American Journal of Sociology* 85 (3) November, pp. 551–573.

Hochschild, Arlie Russell. 1983. *The Managed Heart: Commercialization of Human Feeling.* Berkeley, CA: University of California Press.

Homans, George C. 1961. *Social Behavior: Its Elementary Forms.* London: Routledge.

James, William. [1890] 1981. *Principles of Psychology.* Cambridge, MA: Harvard University Press.

Joas, Hans. [1980] 1985. *G. H. Mead: A Contemporary Re-Examination.* Translated by Raymond Mayer. Cambridge, MA: MIT Press.

Joas, Hans. [1995] 1996. *The Creativity of Action.* Translated by Jeremy Gaines and Paul Keast. Chicago: University of Chicago Press.

Kahneman, Daniel. 2011. *Thinking, Fast and Slow.* New York: Farrar, Straus, and Giroux.

Keys, Daniel. 2006. *The Quote Verifier: Who Said What, Where, and When.* New York: St. Martin's Press.

Klinenberg, Eric. 2012. *Going Solo: The Extraordinary Rise and Appeal of Living Alone.* New York: Penguin.

Kuhn, Thomas S. 1959. *The Copernican Revolution: Planetary Astronomy in the History of Western Thought.* Cambridge, MA: Harvard University Press.

Kuhn, Thomas. 1970. *The Structure of Scientific Revolutions: Second Revised Edition.* Chicago: University of Chicago Press.

Kuhn, Thomas. 1977. "The Relations Between the History and the Philosophy of Science." In *The Essential Tension: Selected Studies in Scientific Tradition.* Chicago: University of Chicago Press.

Lamont, Michèle. 2000. *The Dignity of Working Men: Morality and Boundaries of Race, Class, and Immigration.* Cambridge, MA: Harvard University Press.

Lepenies, Wolf. [1968] 1992. *Melancholy and Society.* Translated by Jeremy Gaines and Doris Jones. Cambridge, MA: Harvard University Press.

Leverenz, Brian. 2003. "Best Buzz." *Chicago Athlete Magazine.* July/August: pg. 14.

London, Harvey; Schubert, Daniel S., Washburn, Daniel. 1972. "Autonomic Arousal by Boredom." *Journal of Abnormal Psychology* 80 (1): pp. 26–36.

Mace, John H. 2007. Editor. *Involuntary Memory.* Malden, MA: Blackwell.

Manguel, Alberto. 1997. *A History of Reading.* New York: Penguin.

Martin, Bernice. 1984. "Mother Wouldn't Like It: House Work as Magic." *Theory, Culture and Society* 2 (2): pp. 19–37.

Martin, John Levi. 2009. *Social Structures.* Princeton, NJ. Princeton University Press.

Marx, Karl. [1859] 1973. *Grundrisse: Foundations of the Critique of Political Economy.* Translated by Martin Nicolaus. New York: Random House.

McDam, Daniel. "History of Jigsaw Puzzles." Online at American Jigsaw Puzzle Society. http://jigsaw-puzzle.org/jigsaw-puzzle-history.html. Accessed August 6, 2009.

Mead, George Herbert. [1924] 1964. "The Genesis of the Self and Social Control." In *Selected Writings, George Herbert Mead*. Edited by Andrew J. Reck, pp. 267–305. Chicago: University of Chicago Press.

Mead, George Herbert. 1934. *Mind, Self, and Society from the Standpoint of a Social Behaviorist*. Edited by Charles W. Morris. Chicago: University of Chicago Press.

Mead, George Herbert. [1927] 1934. "Fragments on Ethics." In *Mind, Self, and Society*. Edited by Charles W. Morris, pp. 354–378. Chicago: University of Chicago Press.

Merton, Thomas. 1960. "Notes: A Philosophy of Solitude." In *Disputed Questions*, pp. 177–207. New York: Harcourt Brace.

Miller, David L. 1973. *George Herbert Mead: Self, Language, and the World*. Chicago: University of Chicago Press.

Mische, Ann. 2009. "Prospects and Possibilities: Researching Futures in Action." *Sociological Forum* 24 (3) September, pp. 694–704.

Montaigne, Michel de. [1572–1574] 1958. "Of Solitude." In *The Complete Montaigne*. Translated by Donald M. Frame, pp. 174–183. Stanford, CA: Stanford University Press.

Nisbet, Robert. 1982. *Prejudices: A Philosophical Dictionary*. Cambridge, MA: Harvard University Press.

On-Line Etymology. "Epiphany." Online at http://www.etymonline. com/index.php?term=ephiphany. Accessed August 24, 2011.

Pagis, Michal. 2010. "From Abstract Knowledge to Experiential Knowledge: Embodying Enlightenment in a Meditation Center." *Qualitative Sociology* 33 (4) December, pp. 469–489.

Parsons, Talcott. 1951. *The Social System*. New York: Free Press.

Pope, Alexander. [1700] 1966. "Ode on Solitude." In *The Poems of Alexander Pope*. Edited by John Butt, p. 265. New Haven, CT: Yale University Press.

Proust, Marcel. [1913] 1992. *Swann's way: In Search of Lost Time*. Translated by C. K. Scott Moncrieff and Terrance Kilmartin. Revised by D. J. Enright. New York: Modern Library.

Radkau, Joachim M. [2005] 2009. *Max Weber: A Biography*. Translated by Patrick Camilter. Cambridge, UK: Polity Press.

Rai, Mythili. 2009. "Decades of Beefcakes, Bodies and Harlequin Romances." CNN online at http://edition.cnn.com/2009/LIVING/wayoflife/o6/03/harlequin.romance.novels/index.html. Accessed August 28, 2012.

Raileanu, Lilia. "Indeterminate Waiting." Unpublished manuscript. Department of Sociology, Rutgers University. New Brunswick, NJ.

Rice, Grantland. 1924. "The Four Horsemen." *New York Herald Tribune*. October 18, 1924.

Rivlin, Gary. 2004. "Tug of the Newfangled Slot Machines." *New York Times*, May 9, 2004. Online at http://www.nytimes.com/2004/05/09/magazine/o9SLOTS.html?pagewanted=all. Accessed on August 28, 2012.

Rogers, Mary F. 1991. *Novels, Novelists, and Readers: Toward a Phenomenological Sociology of Literature*. Albany: State University of New York Press.

Rothschild, Emma. 2009. "Can We Transform the Auto-Industrial Society?" *New York Review of Books*, February 26, 2009. Online at http://www.nybooks.com/articles/archives/2009/feb/26/can-we-transform-the-auto-industrial-society/?pagination=false. Accessed August 28, 2012.

Rousseau, Jean-Jacques. [1776] 1979. *Reveries of the Solitary Walker*. Translated by Peter France. New York: Penguin.

Russo, Richard. 1997. "Interview with Ron Holden." Online http://www.beatrice.com/interview/richard-russo.html. Accessed January 13, 2011.

Russo, Richard. "Interview." HBO website. http://www.hbo.com/movies/empire-falls/inside/interviews/interview/richard-russo.html#/. Accessed April 27, 2015.

Sarton, May. 1973. *Solitude in Society: A Sociological Study in French Literature*. Cambridge, MA: Harvard University Press.

Sayre, Robert. 1978. *Solitude in Society: A Sociological Study in French Literature*. Cambridge, MA and London: Harvard University Press.

Schüll, Natasha Dow. 2012. *Addiction by Design: Machine Gambling in Las Vegas*. Princeton, NJ: Princeton University Press.

Schutz, Alfred. [1953] 1982. "Common-Sense and Scientific Interpretation of Human Behavior." In vol. I of *The Problem of Social Reality: Collected Papers*, pp. 3–47, The Hague, The Netherlands: Martins Nijhoff.

Shalin, Dmitri N. 1988. "Pragmatism and Social Interactionism." *American Sociological Review* 51 (1) February, pp. 9–29.

Shalin, Dmitri N. 2000. "George Herbert Mead." In *The Blackwell Companion to Major Classical Social Theorists*, pp. 290–332, Malden, MA: George Ritzer.

Simmel, Georg. [1908] 1950. *The Sociology of Georg Simmel*. Translated by Kurt H. Wolff. New York: Free Press.

Storr, Anthony. 1988. *Solitude: A Return to the Self*. New York: Ballantine.

Sudnow, David. 1981. *Ways of the Hand: the Sociological Organization of Improvised Conduct*. New York: Harper Colophon Books.

Swedberg. 1988. *Max Weber and the Idea of Economic Sociology*. Princeton, NJ: Princeton University Press.

Swidler, Ann. 1986. "Cultural Action: Symbols and Strategies." *American Sociological Review* 51 (2) April, pp. 273–286.

Terkel, Studs. 1972. *Working: People Talk About What They do, How They Do It, and How They Feel About What They Do*. New York: Pantheon.

Thoreau, Henry David. [1854] 1992. *Walden and Resistance to Government*. New York: Norton.

Timmerman, Jacobo. 1981. *Prisoner without Name, Cell without Number*. Translated by Toby Talbot. New York: Knopf.

Vaisey, Steven. 2009. "Motivation and Justification: A Dual-Process Model of Culture in Action." *American Journal of Sociology* 114 (6) May, pp. 1675–1715.

Waite, Terry. 1995. *Footfalls in Memory: Reflections from a Solitude*. London: Hodder and Stoughton.

Weber, Max. 1946. *From Max Weber: Essays in Sociology*. Translated by Hans H. Gerth and C. Wright Mills. New York: Oxford University Press.

Weber, Max. [1904–1905] 1958. *The Protestant Ethic and the Spirit of Capitalism*. Translated by Talcott Parsons. New York: Scribner.

Weber, Max. [1921] 1968. *Economy and Society: An Outline of Interpretive Sociology*. Edited by Guenther Roth and Claus Wittich. New York: Bedminster.

Weil, Simone. [1950] 1977. "Human Personality." In *The Simone Weil Reader*. Translated by Richard Rees, pp. 313–339. Mt. Kisco, NY: Moyer Bell.

Wiley, Norbert. 2006. "Inner Speech as a Language: A Saussurean Inquiry." *Journal for the Theory of Social Behavior* 36 (3): pp. 319–341.

Wiley, Norbert. 2010. "Inner Speech and Agency." In *Conversations About Reflexivity*. Edited by Margaret S. Archer, pp. 17–39. Oxford, UK: Routledge.

Wilson, Timothy. 2002. *Strangers to Ourselves: Discovering the Adaptive Unconscious*. Cambridge, MA: Harvard University Press.

Wrong, Dennis H. 1995. *The Problem of Order: What Unites and Divides Society*. Cambridge, MA: Harvard University Press.

Wrong, Dennis H. [1961] 1976. "The Oversocialized Conception of Man in Modern Sociology." In *Skeptical Sociology*, pp. 31–54. New York: Columbia University Press.

Zambrini, Silvia. 2009. *Nuova Sordita: Rieflessione Attorno Ai Sintomi di una Societa Disttrat*. Trueste: Editioni Goliardiche.

Zerubavel, Eviatar. 1981. *Hidden Rhythms: Schedules and Calendars in Social Life*. Chicago: University of Chicago Press.

Zerubavel, Eviatar. 1997. *Social Mindscapes: An Invitation to Cognitive Sociology*. Cambridge, MA: Harvard University Press.

INDEX